MOOR BORN

Anne, Emily and Charlotte

MOOR BORN

A Play

BY

DAN TOTHEROH

SAMUEL FRENCH

NEW YORK   LOS ANGELES

SAMUEL FRENCH LTD.   LONDON

1934

MANUFACTURED IN THE UNITED STATES OF AMERICA
BY THE VAIL-BALLOU PRESS, INC., BINGHAMTON, N. Y.

FOR HELEN

*Who made this possible
with her courage and faith.*

"MOOR BORN" was first produced by George Bushar and John Tuerk at The Playhouse, New York, April 3, 1934. Following is a copy of the program of the first performance.

GEORGE BUSHAR—JOHN TUERK

OFFER

"MOOR BORN"

A PLAY

BY

DAN TOTHEROH

STAGED BY

MELVYN DOUGLAS

CAST
(IN ORDER OF APPEARANCE)

ANNE BRONTË	Played by	*Edith Barrett*
MARTHA, a young servant ...	" "	*Grace Francis*
TABBY, their old servant	" "	*Beverly Sitgreaves*
CHARLOTTE BRONTË	" "	*Frances Starr*
EMILY BRONTË	" "	*Helen Gahagan*
BRANWELL BRONTË	" "	*Glenn Anders*
REV. PATRICK BRONTË	" "	*Thomas Findlay*
CHRISTOPHER, a Yorkshire farmhand	" "	*Arling Alcine*

The play is in five parts. All scenes take place in the narrow hallway and sitting room of the Parsonage at Haworth, Yorkshire, England.

PART ONE
Late afternoon in the year 1845.

PART TWO
Late that night.

PART THREE
(3 Years Later)
A morning in September, 1848.

PART FOUR
Evening of the same day.

PART FIVE
Three months later, about noon.

PART ONE

The sitting-room of the parsonage at Har-
worth. A late afternoon in the year 1845.
The room is rectangular. A coal-burning fire-
place is in the right wall, a door leading to the
kitchen above it. The rear wall is broken by a
high square double doorway in the center. The
two doors are opened and remain flat against
the wall throughout the play. Two deeply re-
cessed windows, high and each of four feet
width, are in the left wall. Looking through
the doorway, part of the center hallway of the
house is visible. The exterior door (not seen)
is to the left. A straight stairway with heavy
balustrade ends at the center of the door open-
ing and carries off—up to the right. There is
a passage-way below the staircase leading off
right, and in the back hallway wall, (to which
the stairs join) is the door of the REV.
BRONTË'S *study, at the foot of the stairs. A*
grandfather's clock separates the bottom step
from this doorway. Through the windows the
churchyard, choked with gravestones, and the
church is visible with the moor lands stretch-
ing beyond.
Everything about the room, and indeed about
the whole house, tells of the most dainty order,

3

*the most exquisite cleanliness, yet it is bare
and severe. There is just the necessary furni-
ture, nothing really soft and feminine be-
speaking the presence of five women in the
house, such as dainty curtains or frivolous or-
naments on the shelf over the fireplace. There
is a great deal of reading matter on the center
table . . . papers, magazines and books, for
there are minds in this house, ravenous for
enlightenment.*

*The furnishings of the room consist of a sofa
facing front, the right end of which is near-
est the fireplace, a hassock near by and the
REVEREND BRONTË'S arm chair in the extreme
down stage right corner below the fireplace.
A secretary, book laden, occupies the wall
space to the right of the center doorway
while an upright piano stands against the wall
on the left side. A large center table is down
stage slightly left of center with three straight
chairs around it. A fourth chair is in the upstage angle of the back and left wall. Dull
wine-colored cloth drapery hangs from curtain poles at the windows, pushed close to the
casings. The mantel is adorned with a small
clock and two candle lamps are placed on
either side of it. An oil portrait of the three
Brontë sisters by Branwell Brontë hangs
above the clock. Reading matter adorns the
table—books, magazines and newspapers of
the period. A double oil lamp stands on a small
table between the windows. A sewing basket*

*is in the lower recessed window seat. Three
little lap desks (one for each of the Brontë
girls) are used throughout the play by their
owners. As the curtain rises* ANNE, *sitting in
the light from the lower window, is writing
on hers, held on her lap. The desks of*
CHARLOTTE *and* EMILY *are on the table.*

*The room is quite still, except for the scratch-
ing of* ANNE'S *pen, but the moor winds, ever
tireless, sweep against the side of the parsonage and whimper about to explore the cornices
of stone.*

ANNE *is deep in her thoughts. Her wide brow
is furrowed. Suddenly she stops writing and
takes up what she has written, holding it
close to the window, the better to catch the
meager light. She reads a stanza aloud to
sound-out the meter:*

ANNE.

    "I too have smiled, and thought like you,
      But madly smiled, and falsely deemed:
      Truth led me to the present view,—
      I'm waking now . . . 'twas then I dreamed."

[*She pauses for a moment, considering; then she re-
peats the last line:*]

    "I'm waking now . . . 'twas then I dreamed."

[*She puts the poem back on the desk and picking up her
pen is about to make some small correction when*
MARTHA, *a young servant, raw-boned, scarlet-faced,
comes from the kitchen door, carrying a tray of tea*

things. She bears them, without speaking, to the center table, and puts them down, clearing a space by stacking up some of the books and papers.] Oh . . . is it time for tea, Martha?

MARTHA. [*Nodding.*] Nearly five o'clock, Miss Anne.

ANNE. I think we'd better wait just a little while longer.

MARTHA. Ay, Miss Anne, but not too long, or you'll be havin' it for supper. [*She starts to go out.*]

ANNE. Didn't I hear the postman a short time ago, Martha?

MARTHA. [*Tossing her head.*] That I don't know, Miss Anne. You know as well as me that ain't none o' my business.

ANNE. [*Gently reproving her.*] Martha, come here. Martha, are you and Tabby still quarreling about that?

MARTHA. Quarrelin'? Humph, not me, Miss Anne. I let her have her own way, if it pleases her!

ANNE. She's a very old lady, Martha. You must try to be patient with her.

MARTHA. [*Sniffing.*] She acts like she thinks I'd been readin' the letters wot ain't mine, as if I so much as touches one of um.

ANNE. I don't believe that's it. Now that she can't do much of the heavy kitchen work, she likes to make herself useful by doing the little *personal* things for us. You can understand that, can't you, Martha?

MARTHA. Ay, Miss Anne . . . [*At the hall door.*]
Thou'll be callin' me when ye're ready for the tea?

ANNE. Yes, I'll call you. [*She is looking over the poem
again.*]

[*The thin light dims and the shadows in the corners of
the sitting room darken.* MARTHA *goes into the kitchen
and closes the door.* TABBY, *the ancient servant of the
parsonage, comes in through the front door, carrying a
few letters and some magazines. She is tall and stooped
and limps badly. She shuffles along the hall and into the
sitting-room from left, stopping by the center table.*]

TABBY. [*Severely, her accent and tone of speech blunt
and harsh.*] There go ye're eyes agin! Git a lamp,
Miss Anne . . . think ye be a cat to see in th' dark?
Take a heedin' fra yer father. . . . Sich a stubborn
lot . . . [*Her sentences run together in a sort of tooth-
less mumble.*]

ANNE. [*Who cannot refrain from smiling.*] There's
plenty of light yet, Tabby. The sun's still above the
churchyard wall.

TABBY. 'Tain't in here!

ANNE. [*Shaking her head; tenderness in her tone.*]
Maybe not for your eyes, Tabby, but . . .

TABBY. [*Who is quite deaf at times, shuffling closer to
ANNE, one gnarled hand cupped around an ear.*] Wot's
that you say?

ANNE. I said that the sun was strong enough for me.

TABBY. Humph! Don't believe so! Here's some letters.

[*She hands the post to* ANNE, *and remains standing close by.*]

ANNE. [*Looking through the letters hastily and eagerly.*] Not an answer yet.

TABBY. Eh?

ANNE. There are no answers about the school. [*She puts post aside, and picks up her pen.*]

TABBY. Humph . . . I coulda tol' ye that.

ANNE. You're not very complimentary, Tabby.

TABBY. Wot would they be doin' a-comin' here?

ANNE. It might not be a very cheerful place, but think of all the knowledge we could give them! [*She smiles up at* TABBY.]

[TABBY *chooses not to be amused. She wags her head.* ANNE *goes on with her writing. There is a pause.*]

TABBY. Wot be you writin' . . . a letter?

ANNE. [*Placing a hand over the poem.*] Y . . . yes . . . a letter.

TABBY. Not to Miss Charlotte?

ANNE. Hardly to Miss Charlotte, unless I want to place it in her own hands, any moment now.

TABBY. That's wot I thought, but she's late. She mayn't come today.

ANNE. She'll come today. There may not have been a gig handy, she's probably walking from Keighley.

TABBY. Ay. [*Turning.*] Think I'll go see if they be needin' me upstairs.

ANNE. [*Rising.*] Let *me* do that.

TABBY. Noa . . . you keep on wi' yer letters.

ANNE. But you've other things to tend to, and I'm just sitting here, doing nothing.

TABBY. [*Turning on* ANNE, *fiercely.*] Want to take *all* my tasks from me? Why doan't you say I'm o' noa use, an' be done wi' me? Martha an' Miss Emily drives me out o' the kitchen . . . make me feel like I'm dead an' buried under earth an' stone. . . .

ANNE. Tabitha Acroid . . . you ought to be ashamed!

TABBY. [*Rushing on, heedlessly.*] Martha brings in the tea things. . . . Miss Emily makes breead in the mornin's. . . . Wot's left for me?

ANNE. [*Leads* TABBY *to back of table.*] You forget how hard you've worked for us, all these years, Tabby. Now it's time for you to take some rest.

TABBY. [*Snorting.*] Humph! I'll rest mysel' in my grave when I comes to it, but not afore!

[*Both down to back of table.*]

ANNE. Well . . . Emily's still out walking. Perhaps Martha might be needing you in the kitchen. [*Pulling* TABBY *toward center.*]

TABBY. Not her! She wants to do it all hersel'. Anyways, Miss Emily won't be likin' it neither.

ANNE. But she's out walking, who knows when she'll be back?

TABBY. Quar, stubborn un. [ANNE *to fire during this.*] In my day, no creature walked of the moors by theirsels for a-fearin' o' the fairish. They was up to bad tricks, they was . . . an' gels come back daft fra the moors . . . an' wot they churned was sour . . . an' 'tis said they never got a husband.

ANNE. [*With a twinkle.*] Maybe that's the trouble with the Brontë girls.

TABBY. Don't joke abat the fairish, Miss Anne.

ANNE. But there's none left now, Tabby, you've often told us.

TABBY. It wur the factories as had driven 'em away, but there mought be some of 'em left in the becks by moonlight, an' the heather thick enow to hide 'em.

[*She starts up during speech. Wagging her head, she shuffles toward the hall and stairs, but* ANNE *runs before her, into the hall, barring her way at the foot of the stairs.*]

ANNE. I'll go up. You have such trouble climbing the stairs. [*Appealingly.*] Please, Tabby . . . I want to help.

TABBY. Noa . . . they're maybe asleep. You'll sure to wake um.

ANNE. What about yourself? [*She lightly runs up a few steps.*] Can you make less noise than that?

TABBY. [*Shaking her head.*] Ay now, there ye go! An'
I was just after savin' ye trouble. You need the rest,
Miss Anne. You ain't too weel yourself, an' wot you
been through these las' days won't be makin' you no
stronger.

ANNE. That's not to be talked about, Tabby . . . especially in front of Master Branwell.

TABBY. [*Tossing her head.*] I been in this house nigh
on twenty-eight year, an' *you* got to be tellin' me that!

[*She sniffs.*]

ANNE. [*Coming downstairs.*] Now, Tabby, you mustn't
be so sensitive. There's enough of that in this house.
[*She is about to put an arm around* TABBY *to comfort
her when a sound outside attracts her attention.*] That
was a cart stopped outside, Tabby . . . it must be
Charlotte.

TABBY. Eh? Wot? [*She turns, bewildered, for she
hasn't quite caught what* ANNE *said.*] Miss Charlotte?
Where? [*Crosses to upper window. Looks out.*]

ANNE. [*Listening.*] Yes . . . it *must* be Charlotte.

[*She runs out front door. A feminine voice calls some-
one's name. The sound is caught up by the moor wind
and is carried away.* ANNE *calls,* "Charlotte! Charlotte!" TABBY *crosses to center door, standing at foot of
stairway and peering off left. Her coarse skirts are
blown back by the wind. The wind goes whistling
around the parsonage.* TABBY, *shading her eyes with
her hand, peers out into the cold shadows of late after-*

noon. ANNE *and* CHARLOTTE *are heard talking and laughing together but what they say is not understandable at first.* MARTHA *comes to the kitchen door; opens it; peeks into the hall; closes the door again. Voices nearer.* TABBY *shuffles back into the sitting-room and to one side, standing against the wall.* ANNE, *her arm locked in* CHARLOTTE'S *returns through the front door. She carries a small satchel belonging to* CHARLOTTE. CHARLOTTE *carries a larger hand-bag to which an umbrella is strapped. She wears a heavy cape, the high collar buttoned around her throat and a little brown bonnet without ornamentation. Her feet are caked with mud from the road and her rather plain face is flushed from walking. She is a short and rather dumpy woman with tiny hands and feet. Her age is about thirty. Her near-sighted, widely spaced eyes are dark and piercing. Immediately upon entering the sitting-room,* CHARLOTTE *sets down the hand-bag and looks about her, eagerly, happily, as though she has been away from home for a long time and is delighted to be back again.*]

CHARLOTTE. It's so dark in here, Anne. Naughty girl, you've been straining your eyes again. [*Suddenly she sees* TABBY, *who stands in the shadow.*] Tabby . . . [*She goes to her.* TABBY *makes an awkward and quaint little curtsey of respect.* CHARLOTTE *puts an arm around her.*] Are you getting along all right?

TABBY. Ay. . . .

CHARLOTTE. Have you taken good care of my sisters?

TABBY. Ay. . . . [*She steps back from* CHARLOTTE;

looks at ANNE *significantly.*] I'll fetch a lamp. [*She shuffles out; into the kitchen.*]

CHARLOTTE. [*Back to* ANNE *as she unfastens her cloak and takes off her bonnet.*] Are you sure you haven't been straining your eyes?

ANNE. Yes, Charlotte.

CHARLOTTE. Any important letters?

ANNE. No, Charlotte.

CHARLOTTE. No inquiries about our school?

ANNE. No.

CHARLOTTE. Not *one* answer?

ANNE. I'm sorry, Charlotte . . . not one.

CHARLOTTE. [*Shrugging.*] Well . . . I suppose *that* dream's over. [*Hiding her disappointment.*] Where's Emily?

ANNE. [*Who crosses room to poke up the fire in the grate.*] Out walking. She finished the baking early and then went out with Keeper. [*She stoops down to poke the fire.*]

CHARLOTTE. Try to keep Emily indoors when the heather's purple. Is she well?

ANNE. Oh, yes. She had a little cold, but fought it off, and as usual didn't even mention it.

CHARLOTTE. [*Hesitating, as if afraid to ask.*] And . . . and Papa?

ANNE. He's in his room, lying down. [*To left of couch.*]

CHARLOTTE. How are his eyes?

ANNE. Ever so much worse, I think. He can only grope his way about, and last Sabbath he had to be led up to the pulpit. He preached his whole sermon with his eyes fixed on one spot.

CHARLOTTE. Poor Papa. . . .

ANNE. I read the "Edinburgh Review" to him this morning. There was an article about Catholicism which infuriated him.

CHARLOTTE. You should have skipped that.

ANNE. He insisted upon hearing it. I think he rather enjoyed his fit of temper.

CHARLOTTE. You don't have to tell me that.

ANNE. He'll be glad you're back, Charlotte. [*Still poking the fire.*] We're *all* glad you're back.

CHARLOTTE. And I am too. I feel so guilty, Anne.

ANNE. Oh, why should you?

CHARLOTTE. I've been away, having a delightful time, while you and Emily stayed on here with all the responsibility.

ANNE. [*Remaining on her knees before the grate.*] Don't think of that. You needed a change, more than any of us. It *was* nice to be with your friends again, wasn't it? How is Ellen and her family?

CHARLOTTE. In splendid health, all of them . . . and they send their felicitations and affection.

ANNE. I do hope Ellen will visit us soon.

CHARLOTTE. I made her promise she would, but not until later; after Papa's eyes are better and the weather clears. It would be gloomy for her here now.

ANNE. Yes, it would be gloomy.

CHARLOTTE. What else has happened?

ANNE. [*Hesitating. We feel she has more to say but lacks the courage.*] Very little. You know how it is here. [*Smiling.*] Oh, yes, the curates rushed into tea. It was last Monday and we were all tired from baking and washing. We wouldn't have minded so much if we could have served them in peace, but they began glorifying themselves and abusing Dissenters in such a manner that Emily lost her temper. Well, you can imagine what happened.

[TABBY *enters from kitchen carrying lighted lamp. She is followed by* MARTHA *bearing two lighted mantel candles.*]

CHARLOTTE. [*Laughing.*] Did she sweep them all out with a broom?

ANNE. Almost. She didn't say much but she *looked* a great deal. It was funny to see them slink away.

[*The sisters laugh together.*]

MARTHA. Miss Charlotte.

CHARLOTTE. How are you, Martha?

MARTHA. I'm varry weel, Miss Charlotte.

CHARLOTTE. You look blooming as ever.

MARTHA. It's glad I am to see you back again. Might I be servin' the tea now, Miss Anne?

CHARLOTTE. Oh, yes, let's have tea. Are there any cheese cakes?

MARTHA. Miss Emily baked some fresh only yesterday.

CHARLOTTE. Is that naughty of me, Anne . . . cheese cakes after five o'clock?

ANNE. Not after a long journey.

CHARLOTTE. Thank you, Anne. Cheese cakes, Martha.

MARTHA. Varry weel, Miss Charlotte. [MARTHA *exits.*]

[TABBY *putters around putting tea cloth on left end of table.*]

CHARLOTTE. Oh, Anne— [*Seeing* TABBY, *and to get rid of her.*] Tabby, there's something burning in the kitchen.

TABBY. Eh?

CHARLOTTE. I think I smell something burning in the kitchen, you'd better go and see.

TABBY. 'Tain't my business. Let Martha tend to that.

[TABBY *limps up to and sits on chair in upper left corner of room, intently listening to the girls' dialogue.*]

CHARLOTTE. [*Pulling* ANNE *down on the sofa beside her.*] I had such a delightful experience coming back on the train . . . perhaps you'll think it a little unconventional and . . . and bold of me . . . but it *was* delightful.

ANNE. Oh, tell me about it!

CHARLOTTE. Promise me you won't be shocked?

ANNE. I'll try not to be.

CHARLOTTE. Well . . . there was a *gentleman* with me in the railway carriage . . . [*She looks out of the corner of her eye at* ANNE *to get the effect of this remark, but* ANNE *simply nods, her expression unchanging.*] . . . and we hadn't ridden very far before I was certain that he was a *Frenchman.*

ANNE. A Frenchman . . . how exciting! . . . and you talked to him in French?

CHARLOTTE. Yes, in French. I was a bit rusty at first, but after a while it began coming back to me, and before we stopped at Keighley I was jabbering away like a native. He knew Brussels, Anne!

ANNE. What a coincidence!

CHARLOTTE. And the Pensionat of Madame Heger.

ANNE. [*Clasping her hands.*] Really?

CHARLOTTE. Yes . . . and what's more, he had lodgings in the Rue d'Isabelle, only three doors away from the school.

ANNE. Where was he going?

CHARLOTTE. Oh not to Haworth, rest assured, Anne. I'll never see him again.

ANNE. I didn't mean that. Didn't it make you feel just a little bit sad, Charlotte?

CHARLOTTE. Sad? [*Freezing up.*] No, of course it didn't!

ANNE. You loved Brussels.

CHARLOTTE. [*Coldly.*] My duty is here. But I was glad of the opportunity to brush up on my French again. . . . And now I must run up and see Papa. [*She rises and crosses to upper window seat and takes her wraps from* TABBY *who has been holding them.*]

ANNE. [*Rising nervously.*] Wait and have your tea first.

CHARLOTTE. He'll never forgive me if I don't go to him at once. I should have done it the first thing, instead of stopping to talk. . . . [ANNE *crosses above table to* CHARLOTTE.] I'll come right back. [*She picks up her hand-bag and is about to go to the hall door, when* ANNE *crosses to her, quickly, breathlessly.*]

ANNE. Charlotte . . . there's something I must tell you . . . before you go upstairs. [*Catching her breath.*] Branwell's home.

CHARLOTTE. [*Amazed.*] Branwell? Home? . . . Is . . . is he ill again?

ANNE. Yes . . . much worse than last summer . . . but . . . but that isn't the reason he's home.

CHARLOTTE. He was dismissed by the Robinsons!

ANNE. [*Averting her head.*] Yes.

CHARLOTTE. Oh, Anne. Everything seemed to be going along so peacefully. You and Branwell were so happy in your work. Your letters gave us such hope. [*Sits on window seat.*] We thought he had at last found himself. Were you making those letters up?

ANNE. No, we *were* happy. I wrote you the truth *then*. Later I tried to say between the lines what I couldn't bring myself to write. You didn't understand. [*Almost in tears.*] Oh! . . . how can I tell you, Charlotte? I've dreaded this more than you'll ever imagine.

CHARLOTTE. Did they discover his weaknesses? Perhaps they decided he was the wrong influence for their children?

ANNE. No, not that. Worse than that.

CHARLOTTE. Anne.

ANNE. It was . . . it was Branwell's fatal attraction for women. . . . [*Her lips tremble.*] Oh, why couldn't he have fallen in love with some one else!

CHARLOTTE. Who was it, Anne?

ANNE. Mrs. Robinson.

CHARLOTTE. Mrs. Robinson? [CHARLOTTE's *lips become thin, her cheeks pale.*] Why, she's at least twenty years older than Branwell, isn't she?

ANNE. She *is* easily . . . perhaps more.

CHARLOTTE. Did she . . . did she return Branwell's love?

ANNE. I don't know, although Branwell declares now that she did . . . right there at the house, under her husband's very eyes.

CHARLOTTE. When did you learn of this?

ANNE. I wasn't sure about it until Branwell came home. He was upset and took to drink and opium again, but he didn't speak up until a letter came from Mr. Robinson. He flew into a terrible rage and threatened to kill himself with Papa's pistols.

CHARLOTTE. He's done that before.

ANNE. But this was different. You'd have been afraid if you'd been here, Charlotte. When he became calmer he showed me the letter.

CHARLOTTE. What did it say?

ANNE. It said that his actions had been discovered and that from then on he was to cease all communication with any member of the Robinson family.

TABBY. [*Crossing down behind table.*] I wouldna be blamin' Branwell, if I was anybody. It's *her* wot needs blamin' . . . her wot's older . . . a mother o' childer, an' one o' fine folk. [*Exits hallway and upstairs.*]

CHARLOTTE. [*Placing a gentle hand on* ANNE'S *shoulder.*] Poor Anne, how humiliating for you. . . .

ANNE. [*Slowly to sofa. Resigned.*] I've made up my mind not to go back to the Robinsons, even if they should send for me . . . which I'm sure they won't now.

CHARLOTTE. Does Papa know all this?

ANNE. Yes. To see the two of them together—oh, it's tragic.

CHARLOTTE. Of course he takes Branwell's part?

ANNE. He blames it all on Mrs. Robinson.

CHARLOTTE. [*Walking restlessly around the table. With a hint of bitterness.*] Branwell's the only son of this household, Anne . . . don't ever forget that!

ANNE. [*Missing the sarcasm.*] Yes . . . poor Branwell. We must do all we can to help him, Charlotte. Genius is not easy to understand.

CHARLOTTE. [*Pause. Thin-lipped.*] We've forgiven much in him.

ANNE. He is our brother.

CHARLOTTE. I haven't forgotten that. If I could, perhaps I could see clearer. [*She stops pacing and looks at* ANNE, *cold intolerance in her eyes.*]

ANNE. [*Going to* CHARLOTTE.] I'm sorry to greet you with such news as soon as you get home, Charlotte.

CHARLOTTE. I had a feeling something was wrong. Ellen wanted me to stay but something seemed to be pulling me back here.

ANNE. [*Sadly.*] Something *always* pulls us back to

Haworth. [*She turns as we see* EMILY *come into the hall and enter the sitting-room.*] Oh, here's Emily.

[EMILY *is a tall, angular, wind-swept girl, her dark brown hair uncovered and her arms filled with sprays of purple heather. She seems to emanate the wild, un-tamed and brooding spirit of the moors, and there is a deep impenetrable mystery in her dark hazel eyes such as dwells in the moor's far-reaches. She is twenty-six years old.*]

ANNE. Emily . . . Charlotte's here.

CHARLOTTE. Emily, dear . . .

EMILY. [*In a low, vibrant voice.*] Charlotte. [*The two sisters embrace each other.* CHARLOTTE *gives herself freely, impulsively, but* EMILY *remains locked within herself.*] Did you just come?

CHARLOTTE. Yes. I had to walk most of the way from Keighley. Emily, your hands are like ice. You should have worn your shawl. [*Looking down at her feet.*] Go change your wet shoes at once!

EMILY. [*Unheeding the advice which she cannot tol-erate.*] I should have been here to greet you, but it was so glorious on the moors. I walked on, almost as far as the falls beyond Penistone.

CHARLOTTE. [*Glancing at* ANNE.] We knew you'd keep on walking . . . You see, I smelled the heather too.

EMILY. [*Holding up the purple spray.*] Look at it . . . it's never been so thick . . . and the harebells are in carpets.

CHARLOTTE. The grouse are out too, I heard them calling—"Go back— Go back" as I walked along the road.

EMILY. And I saw violets by Sladen beck.

ANNE. [*Charmed.*] Oh, violets? I must see them.

CHARLOTTE. We'll walk tomorrow . . . the three of us . . . if it doesn't rain.

EMILY. [*Simply, as though stating an established fact.*] It will rain tomorrow. [*She moves toward the door to put the heather in water.*]

CHARLOTTE. Listen to the weather prophet!

EMILY. The wind's heavy with rain.

ANNE. [*Seriously.*] Emily knows.

EMILY. Did you have a nice visit with Ellen?

CHARLOTTE. Wonderful! We talked every minute. But that's spoiled now, when I think of what you and Anne were going through here.

ANNE. I . . . I told her, Emily.

EMILY. Keep those days apart from these, Charlotte.

ANNE. Emily's been so brave, Charlotte. [EMILY *glares at* ANNE.] We couldn't have met this . . . terrible thing without her.

EMILY. I've done nothing.

ANNE. Oh, Emily, *nothing* indeed!

EMILY. Nothing more than his sister should. [EMILY *exits to kitchen.*]

ANNE. [*To* CHARLOTTE.] She's nursed him like a baby.

CHARLOTTE. Of course she has.

ANNE. Only last night . . . she went herself to fetch him home from the Black Bull. He was intoxicated and fought her all the way back . . . but he couldn't break Emily down. . . . At last she got him to bed and talked to him quietly until he fell asleep. But afterwards, when the house was quiet, I heard her coughing down here by the fire. I don't think she slept all night.

CHARLOTTE. She never seemed to care about herself.

[MARTHA *enters with tea tray from kitchen.*]

MARTHA. Tea's ready, Miss Charlotte.

ANNE. And here are the cheese cakes.

[MARTHA *exits to kitchen.*]

CHARLOTTE. [*Continuing her conversation with* ANNE.] Her hands were like icy stones now . . . and her shoes . . .

[*From upstairs* REV. BRONTË'S *voice is heard.*]

REV. BRONTË'S VOICE. Branwell! Branwell! Where are you going, Branwell!

VOICE OF BRANWELL. [*From upstairs. Thickly.*] I'm going out. . . .

VOICE OF REV. BRONTË. No, Branwell! I forbid you! Do you hear your father speaking to you? Branwell, where are you?

ANNE. [*Clasping her hands.*] He's going to the Black Bull again. He mustn't. . . . Oh, it's too terrible!

CHARLOTTE. [*Her mouth a thin, straight line.*] Don't, Anne!

[BRANWELL *appears on the stairs, hurrying down, struggling into his jacket. His tawny hair is disheveled and his eyes blaze. He runs past the center door and is stopped by* ANNE *calling.*]

ANNE. [*Mustering up enough courage to speak, frightened by her brother's wild appearance.*] Branwell . . . Charlotte's here.

CHARLOTTE. Branwell . . .

BRANWELL. Hello there, Charlotte . . . had a good visit? [*He crosses to her and takes her hand.*]

CHARLOTTE. Yes, thanks, Branwell.

BRANWELL. You're looking fit . . . yes, very well . . . It did you good to get away from Haworth. [*He crosses slowly toward center door, stops and after pause, continues.*] You know what I'm thinking?

ANNE. [*Eagerly.*] No, Branwell . . . what?

CHARLOTTE. Tell us. . . .

BRANWELL. [*Looking at painting over fireplace.*] I'd like to paint my three sisters again. . . . I'd paint you outdoors this time, the moors all around you . . . hemming you in . . . binding you, almost.

CHARLOTTE. We'll sit for you any time you wish . . .
won't we, Anne?

ANNE. Yes, yes . . . any time. Tomorrow perhaps.

BRANWELL. Not so quickly. Let the spirit move me. I
have many plans. Poems . . . plays . . . novels. You
just wait. Some day I'll surprise all of you. [*Sits right of
table.*] It must be far away from here . . . London
. . . Paris . . . you know . . . a place where my
own kind of people are. You know what I mean, Charlotte . . . there's something pulls at *you*, too . . .
some ambition . . . calls you away. But you're weak,
you always come back. What made you come back this
time?

CHARLOTTE. This is my home. I was glad to come back.

BRANWELL. Glad to come back to this prison?

CHARLOTTE. [*Ignoring his remark.*] Yes . . . glad I
came back to be with you. Anne says you've been
poorly.

BRANWELL. [*In the voice of a martyr.*] I'm done for,
Charlotte.

CHARLOTTE. You? . . . With your genius? And all
these new plans? How can you talk like that?

BRANWELL. Genius? Hoh, that's dead. *She* killed it.

CHARLOTTE. Could a mere *woman* do that to you, Branwell?

BRANWELL. [*Flaring.*] You don't know anything about
it! Don't discuss her. I'm not condemning her. It
wasn't her fault. Her husband's to blame. . . .

CHARLOTTE. Give some thought to us. Can't you see how worried we are? *We* love you, Branwell. And think of poor Papa. All his hopes are centered in you.

BRANWELL. [*In a moment of pity.*] The poor old man and I have had a terrible night of it; [EMILY *enters from kitchen.*] he does his best! But it's all over with me. . . . [*Suddenly whimpering.*] It's *her* fault. . . .

ANNE. But, Branwell, you just said . . .

BRANWELL. [*Still whimpering.*] I said . . .

CHARLOTTE. [*Now pitying him.*] Branwell . . . [*She goes to touch his hand.*]

BRANWELL. [*Backing away from her and almost into* EMILY *who has entered quietly, a moment before, and stands in the doorway.*] Don't touch me! I don't want pity! Don't touch me! [*He turns and sees* EMILY.] And, look here, if *you* ever come for me again . . . disgracing me before my friends, I'll . . . sister or not . . . I'll . . . [*He bares his teeth and raises his fist.* ANNE *gives a little stifled cry.* EMILY *does not move. She stands straight and hard, looking squarely into* BRANWELL'S *face. His fist relaxes and his arm drops limply to his side. His shoulders slump.*] Oh, what's the use . . . [*He starts out.*]

CHARLOTTE. Where are you going, Branwell?

BRANWELL. [*Wheeling back. In doorway.*] Out . . . to visit with some of my friends . . . out of this cold house.

CHARLOTTE. [*Bitterly.*] To the Black Bull tavern, I suppose!

BRANWELL. Yes! Yes! And why not? It's all there is in this God-forgotten place. The only *warm* spot; the only place I can converse with people who understand me . . . and appreciate my talents. . . .

ANNE. *We* appreciate your talents, Branwell.

BRANWELL. [*At door.*] Thanks, Anne . . . but you're only a woman. . . . I can't say to you the things I could say to my friend Brown, for instance.

CHARLOTTE. [*Sneering.*] A grave-digger!

BRANWELL.   Yes . . . grave-digger. . . . Sneer   at him, Charlotte, sneer away. . . . [*Grimly amused.*] He'll bury all of us. . . . He'll throw in the dirt on our faces. . . . He'll lock us in with his spade. . . . That's good, eh, Emily?

EMILY. [*In a level voice.*] You'd better go back upstairs and write it down before you forget it.

BRANWELL. I won't forget it. . . . I'll tell it to Brown. . . . He'll think it's splendid . . . lock us in with his spade. . . . He'll see the point. . . . I can talk to him . . . fine masculine mind . . . strong . . . loyal to the grave.

CHARLOTTE. Yes, the masculine mind! How superior it is, when it speaks through the fog of liquor and opium!

BRANWELL. Don't be a damned prig, Charlotte. You are that, you know. You weren't always, you used to be my friend. . . .

CHARLOTTE. I am still your friend, Branwell.

BRANWELL. Oh no. You've changed—you should be sympathetic, Charlotte. You've suffered through love too . . . your professor in Brussels—

CHARLOTTE. Branwell.

BRANWELL. I know you've written and written, but there have been no answers, have there, Charlotte?

CHARLOTTE. It's disgusting to be in the same room with you.

BRANWELL. Suppose I do drink and take opium? I have good reason, haven't I? [*Tapping his chest.*] Weak lungs, dear Charlotte, like De Quincey and *you* . . . [*Pointing to* CHARLOTTE.] . . . and *you* . . . [*At* ANNE.] . . . and *you.* . . . [*He kisses* ANNE'S *hair.*] [*At* EMILY.] . . . all of us! [*The* GIRLS, *with the exception of* EMILY *recoil.*] Seeds of death in all of us! Ha, ha, ha . . . are you afraid to hear the truth? Well, so am I! I'm living in the blackest hell.

CHARLOTTE. Because you *choose* to live there.

BRANWELL. Listen to her . . . understanding, isn't she, Emily? Oh, Almighty God, what am I wasting my breath for? I'm done with all damned women . . . all of 'em . . . all of 'em. . . . [*As he speaks he plunges into the hall and exits through the front door.*]

CHARLOTTE. [*Shaken, but still determined.*] Branwell!

[*She attempts to follow him, but* EMILY *stops her at the door.*]

EMILY. [*Calmly.*] It will do no good to argue with him. He's *past* that.

CHARLOTTE. But what *can* we do?

EMILY. Don't cross him.

ANNE. [*Who has gone to the upper window.*] He's coming back.

CHARLOTTE. Oh, I hope so.

ANNE. No. . . . He's running across the graveyard. He's gone. . . . [*She turns away from the window.*]

CHARLOTTE. He talks like a mad-man.

EMILY. Try to be patient.

CHARLOTTE. We *must* help him. [*Making an effort to control herself.*] I hardly knew him.

EMILY. I know . . . we should have prepared you.

ANNE. [*Her sensitive lips quivering.*] I tried to, Charlotte . . . but words seemed so useless. And at first he was so rational.

CHARLOTTE. In such a short time to go like this. . . . Oh, that . . . that terrible woman!———

EMILY. We can't blame anyone.

ANNE. They say all geniuses are like that, at times. [EMILY *looks at* ANNE.] Look at Lord Byron! Perhaps out of this will come a great painting . . . or . . . or a great poem.

CHARLOTTE. He seems possessed by some terrible demon.

ANNE. [*Frightened. Looking front.*] Oh, we mustn't think things like that.

EMILY. [*Flashing a look of scorn at* ANNE.] Look out. . . . Anne believes in demons. Her Calvinistic God is always battling with them.

ANNE. Don't poke fun at me, Emily.

[*Then* EMILY *smiles at* ANNE, *tenderly.*]

CHARLOTTE. We *must* find a way to help him . . . **we must!**

ANNE. A way will come.

[*The voice of* REV. BRONTË *is heard calling from upstairs again.*]

REV. BRONTË. Branwell! Where are you? . . . Branwell! [*As the voice becomes louder, he appears on the stairs.*] Anne! Emily!

ANNE. Yes, Papa.

CHARLOTTE. Poor Papa, he's the one who really suffers.

[REV. BRONTË *descends the stairs as rapidly as his blind condition permits, clinging to the banister as he stumbles down.*]

REV. BRONTË. Did Branwell go out?

ANNE. [*Hurrying to his assistance.*] Yes. . . . Let me help you. Don't hurry so . . . you'll fall.

[REV. BRONTË, *guided by* ANNE, *enters the sitting-room. He is a striking-looking man, above the common height, with a nobly-shaped head and erect carriage for one of seventy years. He wears a long black frock-coat and his neck is sunk to his ears in yards and yards of white silk cravat. He is almost blind from cataracts and peers through heavy, lead-rimmed spectacles.*]

CHARLOTTE. [*Running to him.*] Papa . . . [*She embraces him.*]

REV. BRONTË. Charlotte? Is this my daughter Charlotte? I didn't know you'd returned.

CHARLOTTE. I only just came. I was on my way upstairs to see you, when Branwell . . . [*She pauses, confused.*]

REV. BRONTË. Branwell . . . Yes, Branwell . . . Why didn't you stop him? [*His voice cracking.*] You knew he was going to the Tavern, didn't you?

CHARLOTTE. We . . . we thought so.

REV. BRONTË. [*Seized by an uncontrollable rage.*] Then . . . why didn't you stop him? You know what he'll do there . . . he'll drink himself into a stupor . . . and. . . and eat opium, if he can get it. . . . Those villains will give it to him, all right . . . then he'll come home . . . and all night I'll wrestle with him. . . . Branwell . . . Come back, Branwell. . . . Go fetch him, some one . . . Emily . . . Charlotte . . . Oh . . . [*He knocks over chair right of table.*]

CHARLOTTE. Papa . . . don't . . . you'll hurt yourself. . . . [*She takes his arm.*] Come, sit down. We'll go after him. We'll get him to come home, but you must be quiet. Come. . . . [*She leads him to a chair by the fire. He sinks down on it, exhausted.*] There. . . .

REV. BRONTË. [*Putting a hand over his eyes.*] Oh, Charlotte . . . am I a Job that God must try me so?

CHARLOTTE. Are your eyes much worse, Papa?

REV. BRONTË. I don't know . . . but it seems to be lots darker than it was.

CHARLOTTE. That's the cataracts forming. [*Bending over him.*] Can you see my face?

REV. BRONTË. [*Looking at her.*] Hardly at all . . . a mist, Charlotte.

[ANNE *sits above table.* EMILY *looks in fire.*]

REV. BRONTË. You've been away . . . you haven't seen him for some time. How . . . how did he look to you, Charlotte? Did he seem changed?

CHARLOTTE. Not . . . not very much, Papa.

REV. BRONTË. Be truthful with me, daughter.

CHARLOTTE. He's been much distressed. Naturally it tells on him . . . but he'll be all right soon. Won't he, Anne?

ANNE. [*Moves toward them—then back to table.*] Oh, yes . . . I'm sure he will.

CHARLOTTE. You see? . . . And then he'll fulfill his great promise. Have some tea with us, Papa. You must calm yourself. Tomorrow's the Sabbath. There's your sermon, you know.

REV. BRONTË. [*Slowly.*] Daughters . . . never forget that your brother is a genius. There's no sacrifice too big for us to make for him.

ANNE. No, Papa.

CHARLOTTE. We're going to do everything we possibly can for him.

ANNE. [*At right door.*] Martha, bring us some more hot water.

REV. BRONTË. A genius . . . his inheritance from me. I could have done great things . . . you know my poem, "The Vision of Hell" . . . but I gave up my ambitions for my children . . . and I'm not sorry. Oh, but my life's a failure if Branwell fails.

CHARLOTTE. He's unhappy here. Perhaps we should send him away.

ANNE. Perhaps he would like to study in Paris.

REV. BRONTË. I've thought of that . . . but that will take money, Charlotte.

CHARLOTTE. We'll find a way to make lots of money.

ANNE. [*Timidly.*] We . . . we mustn't forget our school.

CHARLOTTE. [*Firmly.*] We must give up that idea. Not *one* person has replied to our circulars.

ANNE. But a thing like that takes time. We're not yet known as teachers.

CHARLOTTE. Let's not deceive ourselves any longer.

[*With bitterness.* EMILY *turns to look at* CHARLOTTE.]
How did we *ever* hope to entice little children to this
gloomy place? Think of pitting their frail bodies against
these moor winds! [*Pointing out the window.*] They'd
be terrified to look at that graveyard choked with tombstones.

EMILY. [*Intensely, like a savage mother defending her
child.*] Let them stay away! This place is not for any
one who is not moor born!

CHARLOTTE. [*Almost frightened by her sister's savage
tone.*] Emily!

EMILY. I, for one, am glad the scheme has failed!

ANNE. Oh, Emily . . . don't. . . .   } [*Spoken*
REV. BRONTË. Come, come, daughter. . . . } *together.*]

EMILY. I never wanted outsiders here. There's a fearsome beauty in this place, but it's not for every one.
Only a chosen few can thrive on it.

CHARLOTTE. Don't flare so, Emily! I know what you
mean and I agree.

EMILY. Then don't renounce this place. It's been a wild
mother to us three. I think you've changed toward it,
Charlotte, but I still walk hand in hand with it. Do you
think I'll cast it off because it retains its honesty?

CHARLOTTE. You misunderstand me.

EMILY. [*Striding to the hall door.*] Don't blame
Haworth and the moors for our failure. The failure's

in ourselves. [*She goes into the dark hall and paces the hallway until end of act.*]

CHARLOTTE. Goodness! I didn't mean . . . } [*Spoken together.*]
REV. BRONTË. What a temper! }

ANNE. I told you, you can't speak against the moors to Emily.

[EMILY *is seen pacing the length of hallway.*]

CHARLOTTE. I didn't mean to hurt her. Why, she cried out as though I had thrown a stone at her.

MARTHA. [*Coming in from the kitchen with jug of water.*] Oh, Miss Charlotte . . . you ain't touched a drop o' tea. [*Feeling the tea pot.*] It's abat stane cald.

CHARLOTTE. We were just going to have some, Martha.

MARTHA. Here's your hot water.

CHARLOTTE. [*Calling.*] Emily! Come have some tea!

[EMILY *does not reply.*]

REV. BRONTË. [*Bowing his head.*] Give me my tea black and bitter, Charlotte. Let it be like brackish water on my tongue. . . . [*Breaking down—when* CHARLOTTE *gets to him with cup and saucer.*] Oh, my son . . . my son. . . .

CHARLOTTE. [*Kneeling beside him.*] Papa, you're not alone. Your girls are with you, too.

ANNE. [*Kneeling on other side of him.*] We'll never leave you, Papa.

[*The moor wind moans about the house.* EMILY *is pacing the dark hall, her arms locked behind her back; her head bowed.*]

THE CURTAIN FALLS

PART TWO

Time: Night: 10:00 P. M.
The parsonage sitting-room. Late that night.
The fire has burned down to a bed of coals in
the small grate. The lamp is lit on the center
table, casting a soft yellow circle of light. Can-
dles burn on mantel.
At Rise: ANNE *sits on sofa, sewing on some*
shirts for BRANWELL.
On the left side of the table sits CHARLOTTE,
writing a letter in her infinitesimal hand, her
face pushed close to the page, since she is so
very near-sighted.
EMILY *is playing the piano.*
The insistent moor winds cry around the
house and the rain, which EMILY *predicted,*
drips from the eaves and smudges the window
panes.
There is silence for a few moments, ANNE
and CHARLOTTE *intent on their work;* EMILY
plays a few bars at the piano, rises abruptly,
and starts pacing back and forth.

CHARLOTTE. [*Finishing her letter and tossing down the*
pen.] There . . . Ellen can't say I haven't been prompt
this time.

ANNE. You've written pages and pages, Charlotte.

41

CHARLOTTE. And yet I haven't told her anything.

ANNE. You didn't tell her about . . .

CHARLOTTE. Branwell? [EMILY *pauses in her walk.*] Only that he's ill and at home. What time is it?

ANNE. [*Glancing over her shoulder at a small clock on the mantel shelf.*] Ten o'clock. Aren't you tired after your long journey?

CHARLOTTE. A little . . . [*Grandfather clock strikes ten.*]

ANNE. Then why don't you go to bed? Emily and I will wait up for him.

EMILY. [*Still walking back and forth.*] Yes, go to bed, Charlotte. We're used to waiting.

CHARLOTTE. [*Shaking her head.*] I couldn't really sleep until I knew he was safe in the house. Perhaps I'd better go find him, Emily.

EMILY. No . . . I tried that, and you heard what he said to me this afternoon.

CHARLOTTE. But he may not come back for hours yet. [*She imagines she hears something.*] What was that sound? Is he coming? [*Crosses to window.*]

EMILY. [*As she still paces.*] It's only the sound of the wind rising.

ANNE. Have you forgotten what the moor wind sounds like, Charlotte?

CHARLOTTE. [*Still peering out.*] Maybe I have . . . there was hardly a murmur of wind in Ellen's valley.

ANNE. [*Wistfully.*] At Robinson's, too . . . the nights were often still.

EMILY. [*As if speaking to herself.*] I'd *hate* that. . . .

[*A pause. The rain beats down.*]

ANNE. Listen to the rain . . . and Branwell isn't dressed for it.

CHARLOTTE. [*Turning away from the window and standing with her back to it, looking at* EMILY.] Emily, I've been thinking . . . there's Aunt's legacy . . . we could use that to send Branwell away.

ANNE. [*Brightening.*] Why, yes . . . we *could* use some of that!

EMILY. No! He'd only dissipate it, then we'd be worse off than before.

[EMILY *walks continually.*]

CHARLOTTE. But he *should* go away.

EMILY. He's better here . . . in his prison-house, as he calls it.

ANNE. [*Perplexed.*] Oh, Emily . . . do you *think* so?

CHARLOTTE. I don't agree. We should give him every chance. Then there's Papa to be considered. He can't stand this strain much longer . . . and *you,* Emily

. . . you're as nervous as a cat. I don't believe you've sat down all evening.

EMILY. It's *you* who are nervous and unhappy. *You're* the one who should leave this prison-house.

CHARLOTTE. I?

EMILY. Yes, *you.*

CHARLOTTE. Just because of what I said this afternoon?

EMILY. Not only that . . . [*Coming down to the table.*] Who was it came away from school in Brussels with regrets? Not *I,* surely.

CHARLOTTE. I admit it, Emily . . . I saw a chance to better myself. Haven't *you* ambitions, other than the making of bread . . . sweeping floors and walking on the moors?

EMILY. If I have, I don't torture myself with them, as you are doing.

CHARLOTTE. Don't tell me you're content, Emily. That would be unthinkable.

EMILY. How do I know what I am? But if there's contentment any place on earth for me, it's *here* . . . in Haworth. I'd hate those shut-in valleys you and Anne admire.

ANNE. [*Who will be loyal.*] I only liked the change, Emily.

CHARLOTTE. Let's not quarrel about our likes and dislikes. I'm only trying to find the best way out. We have

to admit that a school is impossible in Haworth. Emily
says we shouldn't touch Aunt's legacy. Well then, what's
left? Shall we go away to teach again?

ANNE. We *must,* Charlotte! Papa's almost blind . . .
he'll have to have that operation soon. We must *make*
something of ourselves.

EMILY. [*Looking over her shoulder at* ANNE.] You
too, Anne?

ANNE. [*Confused.*] I mean . . .

CHARLOTTE. You mean we should have careers, Anne?

[*Pause.*]

EMILY. [*Sarcastically.*] Perhaps the *stage!*

ANNE. [*Blushing.*] Oh, no . . . I didn't mean careers
. . . that's for Branwell. . . . We're only women . . .
I meant . . . we shouldn't be idle, that's all.

CHARLOTTE. I suppose we should marry and have children. That's the normal woman's career.

EMILY. [*Stopping by the window.*] Charlotte . . . I
believe you really mean that.

ANNE. [*Laughing.*] Oh, she doesn't!

CHARLOTTE. Would it be such an unheard-of thing to
wish for love and . . . and children?

EMILY. [*Triumphantly.*] You see!

ANNE. [*Eagerly.*] Oh, Charlotte, tell us . . . did you
meet some one at Ellen's . . . some one you could

. . . could . . . [*She pauses, confused, feeling* EMILY'S *eyes on her.*]

EMILY. [*Grimly.*] Say it, Anne . . . don't be afraid of the word!

CHARLOTTE. [*Pugnaciously.*] Love! That's the shameful word you mean . . . *Love!* [*Shaking her head.*] No, dear Anne, I found no one at Ellen's, or any place else.

EMILY. How tragic! The strange and sexless Brontë sisters who can find no one to love them!

ANNE. Tabby blames it on the fairish. She says we're a-cursed from walking alone on the moors . . . *you* especially, Emily.

EMILY. [*In lowered voice.*] I've heard of stranger things than that.

ANNE. Oh, come, Emily . . . don't be so serious. I was only joking.

CHARLOTTE. Oh, let's *not* joke! This is hardly the time for joking. *I,* for one, shall not live on like this. We aren't peasant louts. We're people of intelligence, with wills to fight for something better.

ANNE. We've come through other tragedies.

CHARLOTTE. Let's first agree on this. . . . Do we admit that Branwell is a genius?

ANNE. [*Emphatically.*] Oh, yes!

EMILY. He's painted well enough.

CHARLOTTE. He's painted *very* well. Everybody says his portrait of the three of us is a splendid likeness.

ANNE. He's written too . . . very little lately . . . but before . . .

CHARLOTTE. And there's no reason why he can't write again, with us to help him.

ANNE. Don't you think so, Emily?

EMILY. Oh . . . let him find his own way!

ANNE. Emily!

CHARLOTTE. You don't *really* mean that, Emily.

ANNE. Not after what you've done for him already.

EMILY. I tell you, I've done nothing. [*A pause.* EMILY *suddenly starts; her keen ears have heard something other than the wind.*] Hush . . . he's coming now.

[*She is by the table, and not thinking, she flings down the note-book she has been carrying; snatches up the lighted lamp from the table and goes quickly and silently to the hall door. Above the wind is heard* BRAN-WELL'S *voice, high-pitched and hoarse. He is singing an obscene ballad of the period, although the words cannot be heard plainly.* EMILY *goes into the hall and pauses again, holding the lamp above her head. She listens for a moment. The lamp flares in the wind.*]

BRANWELL'S VOICE. "In a box of the stone jug I was born,
Of a hempen widow the kid forlorn. . . ."

CHARLOTTE. The wind will blow out the lamp, Emily.

EMILY. I'll set it here . . . on the stairs. [*She sets lamp down on the stone stairway.*]

BRANWELL'S VOICE. [*Nearer.*] Oh, fol-de-rol-de-ri . . . Ohhhhhh . . .

ANNE. Oh, stop him before he wakes up Papa!

[EMILY *goes out. The sitting-room is now lit, vaguely, by the coals of the fire in the grate.*]

CHARLOTTE. [*At the window, shading her eyes, as before.*] I can't see him . . . the rain smudges the glass. There comes Emily. Shouldn't I go and help her?

ANNE. [*Crosses to upper window.*] No, she'd be angry if you did. Besides, *she's* the only one who can manage him. Look . . . he's trying to break away from her.

CHARLOTTE. He's striking her!

[ANNE *goes to* CHARLOTTE. CHARLOTTE *makes an abrupt move to go out.*]

ANNE. [*Catching her arm.*] No . . . no . . . wait! He's coming with her now. Look, he's like a child with her.

BRANWELL'S VOICE. Oh, fol-de-rol-de-rollo-oooo. . . . [*He staggers through the front door and into the hall, leaning on* EMILY *who holds him steadily. He stops and pulls away.*] Let go my arm, Emily . . . think I can't walk by myself? Think I'm a baby? *Spoken in hall*

[*He laughs, thickly and mirthlessly, and takes a few wavering steps toward the sitting-room door.* BRAN-

WELL *appears in door.* EMILY *stands at foot of stairs with lamp.*] H . . . how's that? [*Singing.*] Oh . . . on a tavern floor I lay me down. . . .

EMILY. [*Sternly.*] Hush! Don't wake your father!

BRANWELL. My father? Ah, yes, my father . . . the poor old man . . . I dare say he's heart-broken over me, Emily . . . his only son. . . . I admit I give the old man lots of trouble . . . but what does *he* know? . . . I have a sorrow . . . no one knows how deep . . . [*He enters the sitting-room and strikes a tragic attitude in the doorway.*]

EMILY. Branwell, you must go to bed at once! [EMILY *starts a step upstairs.*]

BRANWELL. To bed? . . . Don't be silly. . . . What do I want to go to bed for? . . . To toss all night in black anguish . . . to dream only of her? . . . No, no . . . I won't go to bed. . . . [BRANWELL *backs into room. As though he has just discovered* ANNE *and* CHARLOTTE.] Ah, my sisters . . . behold your brother!

[*He makes a low bow to them and almost falls.* EMILY *has entered and puts lamp on table.*]

CHARLOTTE. Branwell. . . . [*She cannot keep the disgust from her voice.*]

BRANWELL. [*Regaining his balance, crosses to sofa.*] Yes, behold your brother . . . the pride of the Brontës . . . feeling warm now . . . warm and hearty . . . filled with good cheer . . . Black Bull tavern . . . Saw my friend Brown there . . . Brown, the grave-digger . . . splendid fellow. [*Impishly.*] Gave him your regards, Charlotte . . . [*Looking at* CHARLOTTE *through squinted eyes; swaying on his feet.*] Oh, I know I'm a loathsome sight to you, Charlotte, unspeakable, vile villain . . . Why don't you say what you're thinking? Your brother's become an abomination . . . Wash your hands of him . . . he's hopeless . . . hopeless. . . .

CHARLOTTE. Not *hopeless*, Branwell.

BRANWELL. [*Sneering.*] Oh, I can be *saved*, can I? [*Pulls himself up to a squatting posture on sofa.*] My virtuous sister will save me! Pah! Not you . . . not anybody . . . I'm done for . . . done for . . . wrecked by a divine angel with the black heart of Lucifer . . . [*Sobbing, he rolls over on sofa, face down.*]

EMILY. [*Putting a steady hand on his shoulder.*] Stop saying such things and come to bed. You'll feel differently after you've had some sleep.

BRANWELL. Sleep? Did you say sleep? What are you talking about? I tell you I can't *sleep* . . . no sleep . . . only frightful nightmares . . . Her husband . . . he tries to kill me . . . and she . . . she helps him. I run away . . . I scream . . . He shoots a pistol . . . I feel blood . . . She only laughs . . . like a beautiful fiend . . . she laughs . . . at me . . . At me . . . at me . . . and I love her so! [*Pounding sofa.*]

EMILY. [*Speaking through tight lips, her voice like a sword.*] Branwell! Did you hear what I said to you? Come with me! [*She pulls him to a sitting position.*]

BRANWELL. [*Squirming.*] Let me go! . . . You're too damned strong for a woman! Let me go!

EMILY. I'll not let you go! You're coming with me . . . right now! Right now! [*She pulls him sharply.*]

BRANWELL. No . . . no . . . I'm afraid to sleep . . . No . . . No! [*She gets him to his feet.*]

EMILY. Right now!

[*Suddenly* BRANWELL *ceases to struggle. He is completely dominated by* EMILY.]

BRANWELL. [*Slumping.*] Oh . . . what's the use? . . . You win, old girl . . . No use. . . .

[*He goes into the hall with* EMILY. EMILY *helps him up the stairs. They go up slowly.* BRANWELL *mumbles incoherent words. They pass out of sight.*]

ANNE. [*Heaving a deep sigh.*] Now he'll be all right until tomorrow. That's the way it's been ever since he came back.

CHARLOTTE. This *cannot* go on!

ANNE. [*Listening.*] I hope he doesn't awaken Papa.

CHARLOTTE. He's killing us . . . *all* of us! [*Crosses to behind table.*]

ANNE. Papa needs his rest.

CHARLOTTE. We *must* send him away from here.

ANNE. Do you know what I think, Charlotte? Emily really doesn't want to let Branwell go. She's like a

mother with a sick child . . . afraid to let him out of
her sight.

CHARLOTTE. Perhaps . . . but she's dreadfully wrong.
Those awful people at the tavern . . . he must not see
them any more. [*She brushes her fingers along the
table and encounters* EMILY'S *note-book. She picks it
up.*] What's this, Anne?

ANNE. Oh, that? It belongs to Emily. She writes in it,
now and then. [*As* CHARLOTTE *opens the book.*] Oh, I
wouldn't look at it, if I were you. Emily won't like it.
You know how she is. She'll be very angry.

CHARLOTTE. [*Holding the book up close to her near-
sighted eyes.*] Why . . . this is . . . Why, it's poetry,
Anne.

ANNE. Poetry? . . . Oh . . . [*In a flutter.*] . . . it's
no more than I expected but . . . but don't read it,
Charlotte. Put it down before Emily comes back.

CHARLOTTE. [*Unheeding.*] It's very beautiful, Anne
. . . strange and beautiful . . . Listen to this:

> "Well, let them fight for honor's breath,
>   Or pleasure's shade pursue . . .
>   The dweller in the land of death
>   Is changed and careless too.
>
>   And if their eyes should watch and weep
>   Till sorrow's source were dry,
>   She would not, in her tranquil sleep,
>   Return a single sigh."

[CHARLOTTE *looks up, her eyes sparkling with the ex-*

citement of a great discovery.] That's . . . that's great
poetry, Anne!

ANNE. [*Breathlessly, clasping her hands.*] It *is,* isn't
it? And Emily . . . *our* Emily wrote it! . . . [*Then
almost frightened.*]But . . . but don't read any more,
Charlotte . . . [*Tries to take book from* CHARLOTTE.]
. . . please don't . . . You mustn't . . . She'll never
forgive you.

CHARLOTTE. [*Turning a page.*] Oh, listen . . .
  "No coward soul is mine
  No trembler in the world's storm-troubled
    sphere" . . .

[CHARLOTTE *looks up.*] That's Emily, speaking of herself, at last.

ANNE. [*Repeating.*] "No coward soul is mine" . . . It
is Emily. Is there more?

CHARLOTTE. Not of that one. She's scratched something out. [*Turning another page.*] But here she
says . . .

[ANNE *hears* EMILY *coming down the stairs.*]

ANNE. Oh, put it down quickly! She's coming . . . I
beg of you, Charlotte!

CHARLOTTE. Do you think I'd leave such poetry un-
recognized?

ANNE. [*Trembling.*] But that's the last thing Emily
would want. You know that as well as I do. Oh, put it
down, and don't tell her you read it. Please don't!

CHARLOTTE. [*Determined.*] I know what I'm doing, Anne. [*To herself.*] And yet she wants us to believe she's contented with her life here.

[EMILY *enters.* CHARLOTTE *clasps the note-book tightly.* ANNE *quickly crosses to sofa, sits and picks up sewing to cover embarrassment.* EMILY *has remembered her note-book and starts for the table to get it.* ANNE *speaks quickly, attempting to distract her.*]

ANNE. Emily . . . did he . . . did he awaken Papa?

EMILY. [*Turns and looks toward stairway.*] Papa was already awake. You know he doesn't sleep until Branwell comes home.

ANNE. Oh, I'm so sorry. He'll be in a state, and tomorrow's the Sabbath.

CHARLOTTE. [*Holding out the note-book.*] Emily . . . I found this on the table. It's yours, isn't it?

EMILY. [*Crosses quickly to* CHARLOTTE.] Yes . . . I was looking for it. [*She snatches book from* CHARLOTTE.]

CHARLOTTE. They're wonderful, Emily.

EMILY. [*Her brow darkening; her body suddenly stiff and hard.*] You *read* them!

CHARLOTTE. Only . . . here and there . . .

EMILY. You *dared!* [*Holding the book against her breast.*] What *right* had you to read them?

CHARLOTTE. [*Hurt.*] I . . . I didn't intend to . . .

but when I saw the opening lines I couldn't help but finish them. They swept me off my feet.

EMILY. They're mine . . . my very own . . . Written for myself. You had no right to read them!

CHARLOTTE. But . . . but why should you keep such beautiful things to yourself?

EMILY. I feel that way. Need I give a reason?

CHARLOTTE. You can't keep a great gift like that.

EMILY. It's *my* gift!

CHARLOTTE. Gifts like that should be shared with others.

EMILY. You've spied on me, Charlotte!

CHARLOTTE. I didn't mean to.

EMILY. You've done a thing I'd be ashamed to do.

[*Swings down—crosses to fire.*]

CHARLOTTE. How stubborn you are! But from now on, you can't ever tell me you're not ambitious.

EMILY. [*Contemptuously.*] Ambitious! Ambitious for what? They come to me from some unknown source. I write them down to please myself . . . and myself *alone*.

CHARLOTTE. That's a true poet speaking.

EMILY. Certainly they're no different or important than the silly songs I sing to myself when I walk alone on the moors. Who hears them there or cares? Nothing but the curlew and the grouse and they get frightened and fly away! [*She squats on the hassock before the grate, her back turned rigidly to* CHARLOTTE *and* ANNE.]

ANNE. [*To* CHARLOTTE.] You *see?* [*She is much distressed.*]

[*A pause. The wind moans and the rain falls.*]

CHARLOTTE. Emily. [EMILY *does not reply.*] Would it make any difference if I told you that *I've* been writing poems too?

ANNE. [*Breathlessly.*] *Really,* Charlotte?

CHARLOTTE. Yes. [*Inaudibly.*]

EMILY. [*Bitterly.*] But *you're* ambitious.

CHARLOTTE. Why do you hate that word so much? I know . . . it's because you're shy . . . afraid of the world and what the world might say about you. Isn't that it? But *you* needn't be afraid, Emily. I can't believe a mind like yours is without *some* spark of honorable ambition.

EMILY. [*Keeping her back turned, her resentful eyes fixed on the bed of coals.*] Let me alone, Charlotte . . . [*A quiet threat in her voice.*] Let me alone, or . . .

CHARLOTTE. [*Displeased.*] You're as stubborn as Papa or . . . or Branwell.

ANNE. [*Calling, hesitatingly.*] Charlotte . . . Charlotte, don't laugh at me . . . but I've been writing poems too. . . .

CHARLOTTE. You?

ANNE. Just . . . just *little* things.

CHARLOTTE. Anne! You? How exciting! The three of us . . . and we never told each other. Did you hear that, Emily? Anne's guilty too.

[EMILY *shrugs her shoulders but does not reply.*]

ANNE. [*In a nervous flutter.*] Oh . . . but . . . but I'm like Emily, Charlotte. . . . They're just written for myself . . . little things . . . thoughts that come to me. It's a relief to write them down.

CHARLOTTE. [*Who is shaping an idea.*] May I see some of them, Anne?

ANNE. Oh, they're of no consequence . . . only . . . only little things.

CHARLOTTE. That's what Emily thinks of hers.

ANNE. Oh, mine are nothing like Emily's.

CHARLOTTE. Let me judge that. You *will* let me see them, won't you?

ANNE. Why . . . why yes . . . if it would give you pleasure. . . . And then you must let me see yours.

CHARLOTTE. I shall. Go get them, Anne. I have a good reason for seeing them now.

[ANNE *rises, goes to the piano, opens her desk which rests on top of it and takes out a sheaf of poems.*]

CHARLOTTE. Emily, don't sit there like a stone. Don't you know that something wonderful has happened?

Think of it . . . the three of us, all writing in this little house . . . and we didn't even suspect each other. . . . Emily! [*She cries out suddenly, for* EMILY *has put her note-book on the coals.*]

[CHARLOTTE *runs to the grate and speaks as she snatches the note-book from the grate before it has time to catch fire.*] Oh, Emily, you tried to burn them! That's wicked of you!

EMILY. [*Rising.*] They're mine. . . . I can burn them if I wish.

CHARLOTTE. [*Holding them away from* EMILY.] Not *these.*

EMILY. Give them to me, Charlotte!

CHARLOTTE. Not if you're going to destroy them.

EMILY. Give them to me!

CHARLOTTE. Promise me you won't burn them.

EMILY. Give them to me!

CHARLOTTE. Promise first.

EMILY. I promise nothing. . . . Give them to me!

CHARLOTTE. Oh, Emily . . . don't you see what I want to do? We can make a book of our poems . . . poems by the three of us. Who knows? It might be a way out of all our miseries!

ANNE. [*Eyes dancing.*] You mean . . . to publish them, Charlotte?

CHARLOTTE. Yes . . . the best of all we've written in one volume. It came to me like a vision. Poetry's read a great deal these days. The book might make us rich.

EMILY. [*With a sneer.*] And *famous!*

CHARLOTTE. Yes, *and* famous! Why, your poems alone, Emily . . .

EMILY. You shan't publish them.

CHARLOTTE. Oh, Emily!

ANNE. [*Disappointed.*] Emily . . . please . . .

EMILY. [*Witheringly to* ANNE.] I'd as soon walk naked through the streets of Haworth.

ANNE. [*Flushing.*] Well . . . well, I felt like that too . . . only now . . . you see . . . I think Charlotte may be right. This may solve our problem.

CHARLOTTE. Wouldn't you do this for Papa, Emily?

ANNE. And for *Branwell,* Emily?

CHARLOTTE. [*Clutching at this.*] Yes, more for Branwell than any one else. Think of how we can help him with the money when it comes. I *know* you'll do it for Branwell, Emily.

EMILY. [*Shaking her head.*] He'd never forgive us.

CHARLOTTE. What do you mean?

EMILY. How do you think he'd feel to see his sisters' names on a volume of published poems?

CHARLOTTE. You mean he'd be jealous?

EMILY. Might as well strike him across the face with a whip and laugh while you were doing it.

CHARLOTTE. [*After a thoughtful pause.*] He need never know about it.

ANNE. He couldn't help but find it out, Charlotte.

CHARLOTTE. Not if we publish under different names.

ANNE. [*Hopefully.*] We *could* do that, you know.

CHARLOTTE. I have it! We'll be three brothers.

ANNE. That *would* be best! Women aren't thought much of in letters.

CHARLOTTE. We'll *command* their attention that way. Three unknown brothers from Yorkshire.

ANNE. [*Amused.*] That will fool every one. What name shall we take?

CHARLOTTE. [*After a moment's thought.*] Brontë . . . B . . . B? . . . Bell! Why not the three Bells? . . . That's it . . . Bell! I'll be *Currer* Bell. What will you be, Anne?

ANNE. Bell . . . Anne Bell . . . A—A—A—[*Pause —thoughtfully.*] *Acton.* . . . Do you like *Acton* Bell?

CHARLOTTE. Why, yes . . . Acton Bell. And *you,* Emily?

EMILY. [*Who stands with head bent, arms locked behind her back at window.*] What? . . .

CHARLOTTE. What name will *you* take? Anne has chosen Acton . . . and I am Currer Bell.

EMILY. Oh . . . I don't know.

CHARLOTTE. But you agree to do it, don't you?

EMILY. Agree?

CHARLOTTE. Yes . . . for Branwell's sake.

EMILY. Are you sure it's only for Branwell's sake?

CHARLOTTE. Yes . . . what else?

EMILY. Not for any glory of our own?

CHARLOTTE. Oh, Emily . . . must we go all over that again?

ANNE. Say you'll agree, Emily.

CHARLOTTE. I give you my word . . . no one will know.

EMILY. Have your own way, Charlotte, have your own way.

ANNE. Oh, we *are* going to do it then?

CHARLOTTE. It *seems* to be a way out, Anne.

ANNE. [*Shyly.*] Then . . . then would you care to see my poems?

CHARLOTTE. Thank you, Anne. Where are they?

ANNE. [*Hands the poems to* CHARLOTTE.] The one on top I was writing today, before you came home.

CHARLOTTE. Oh, yes. . . . [*She reads aloud.*]

"I too have smiled, and thought like you,
　But madly smiled, and falsely deemed:

Truth led me to the present view,
I'm waking now . . . 'twas then I dreamed."

ANNE. You see . . . it's not much.

CHARLOTTE. Yes it is. . . . It's lovely, Anne. Isn't it, Emily?

EMILY. [*With a tender glance at Anne.*] Yes.

ANNE. That's only one stanza of a very long poem. I call it my views of Life. [*As* CHARLOTTE *turns a page.*] Don't read any more aloud now. Read them later . . . to yourself.

CHARLOTTE. Very well. [*She turns to* EMILY *who stands in front of the fire, one foot on the fender, her arms locked tightly behind her back.*] Come, Emily, don't still be resentful.

EMILY. What do you want me to do?

CHARLOTTE. We must start to plan our publication.

[ANNE *puts poems back in desk.*]

EMILY. That's your task.

CHARLOTTE. Oh no—all three of us must agree. Let's blow out the lamp and walk awhile, arm in arm, as we used to walk here when we were children.

ANNE. Oh let's. We haven't walked that way in years.

CHARLOTTE. Do you remember when we chose our islands, Emily? It was always the Isle of Arran for you.

ANNE. And do you remember when we chose our he-

roes—you picked the Duke of Wellington for yours,
Charlotte. I chose Sir Henry Halford, and Emily's
choice was Walter Scott.

CHARLOTTE. We settled the affairs of a Nation then.

ANNE. And planned our plays . . . but they were just
in fun. We're serious now.

CHARLOTTE. The Bells have work to do. Come, let's get
at it.

ANNE. But you said you were tired tonight.

CHARLOTTE. Tired? How *could* I be tired now?

[*Arms linked, they begin a slow pacing, around the
little room, their heads bent, their brows furrowed in
deep thought like ruminating old men. The wind soughs
around the parsonage. The rain drives against the windows.*]

CHARLOTTE. Of course, unknown as we are, we must
be prepared to publish the book ourselves, but after
that . . .

ANNE. Recognition will come.

CHARLOTTE. And then money. . . .

[*A great blast of wind from the moors rattles the front
door. The coals blink in the grate. The three girls pace
on.*]

CHARLOTTE. Printing isn't cheap, but it will pay to have
the type big and clear. . . .

[*A blast of wind strikes the house. The girls pause,
looking upstage.*]

ANNE. [*Stopping.*] Listen . . . was that only the wind?

[*The three girls listen. Voices, indistinct, come from over their heads.*]

CHARLOTTE. Voices . . .

EMILY. It's Papa, trying to get Branwell to sleep. [EMILY *leaves the others, goes to foot of stairs and looks upward.*]

[CHARLOTTE *and* ANNE *continue their walk.*]

CHARLOTTE. [*In a delighted whisper.*] Little do they know what's going on down here, . . . rich and famous.

[*They pace again, as before. The moor wind rises.*]

ANNE. Oh, Charlotte . . .

THE CURTAIN FALLS SLOWLY

PART THREE

Haworth Parsonage. The year 1848.
The sitting-room again. A morning in Septem-
ber. Cold autumn winds are beginning to
blow over the moor-crest, but there is weak
sunlight trickling through the brightly pol-
ished window panes. The inevitable small fire
burns in the grate.
MARTHA *is up rear of room, using a broom*
on the stones.
TABBY *shuffles in through the front door*
along the hall and then into the sitting-room,
her old arms laden down with mail—papers,
books, magazines and letters. Half-way
across the sitting-room, she drops some of
the mail and MARTHA *comes to her assistance.*

MARTHA. Only yesterday it was, I tol' you you'd better
be lettin' me help ye wi' it. [*Picking up some letters.*]
Doan't ye be sich a stubborn un, Tabby. . . . *You* can't
manage it all, an' every day there be more o' it.

TABBY. [*Putting down her burden on the center table,*
adding it to a vast confusion of other books, papers
and letters.] Put it down here an' go on back to yer
broom! [*She is furious.*]

MARTHA. [*Sorting out the letters she has picked up as*
she crosses to the table, reading aloud.] Currer Bell . . .

Currer Bell . . . Ellis Bell . . . Currer Bell . . . Currer . . . [*Shaking her head.*] Bell . . . Acton Bell
. . . Currer . . . Humm, right quar it 'tis.

TABBY. There ye be, pryin' a nose into wot ain't no con-
cern o' yours.

MARTHA. [*Resentfully.*] I be lookin' fer post o' me
own. I ken get letters fra hame, sometimes, doan't I?
[*She slams the letters down on the table and goes back
to her sweeping, raising a great deal of unnecessary
dust.*]

[TABBY, *mumbling to herself, stacks up the letters, with
clumsy pride and affection, into a neat pile, doing the
same with the papers and magazines.*]

TABBY. [*Words coming out of her mumbling.*] An'
iffen ye go tellin' folks in Haworth anything wot
seems quar to ye in this house, why ups ye'll be packin',
Miss, quicker'n a cat wink!

MARTHA. Who's been sayin' I hev?

TABBY. I'm jest by way o' warnin' ye.

MARTHA. [*Pertly tossing her head.*] A body wot leaves
eyes in potatoes so as folks got to be peelin' um all over
again afterwards, needn't go abat advisin' an' warnin'.

TABBY. Eh? Wot remark was that, Miss?

MARTHA. [*Plying her broom, fiercely.*] Nuthink!

[EMILY *enters from the kitchen with a brown crock
of water. She crosses to the window-seat and begins
watering a potted plant which is on the window sill.*]

TABBY. [*On her way out to the kitchen.*] Miss Emily
. . . the post's just come. . . .

EMILY. [*Pinching off some dry leaves from the plant.
Speaking indifferently.*] Miss Charlotte attends to that.

[TABBY *exits into kitchen.*]

MARTHA. [*Finishing with her broom.*] Can't I be
helpin' ye, Miss Emily?

EMILY. [*Still busy with the plant.*] No, Martha. . . .
Help Tabby. . . .

MARTHA. [*Almost gritting her teeth.*] Her? . . .
That's wot I'm complainin' on. . . . She won't
never . . . [*But as* EMILY *is not paying attention, she
gives up, and mumbling something dark to herself,
starts toward the hallway.*]

[CHARLOTTE *and* ANNE *enter from the kitchen. They
wear quaint house-caps and kitchen aprons.*]

CHARLOTTE. Didn't I hear the postman, Martha?

MARTHA. Ay, Miss Charlotte . . . [*Pointing to table.*]
there ye have it. [*She exits to kitchen.*]

ANNE. Look. . . . Look . . . heaps of it . . . more
and more! [*Clasping her hands, her face flushed.*]
Look, Emily!

[EMILY *does not turn from the window.*]

CHARLOTTE. [*Sorting over the pile of letters.*] Let's see
if we can find the "Quarterly Review." There's supposed to be an illuminating article about the three Bells
in that.

[ANNE *places a chair right of table.*]

ANNE. [*Looking over the magazines and newspapers.*] There're articles in most everything now. [ANNE *dusts sofa.*]

CHARLOTTE. Look at all the letters, Emily! The whole world is coming to little Haworth. [*She hovers over the table, excited.*] Here's some letters for Ellis Bell. . . . [*As* EMILY *does not answer.*] Ellis! [*Laughing.*] Ellis, have you forgotten that's you, Emily? Here, take them. [EMILY *turns and comes down to the table, leaving her crock of water beside the plant on the sill. She takes the letters and puts them in the pocket of her apron, without looking at them.*] And here's one for you, Anne . . . I mean Acton.

ANNE [*Excited.*] Oh! I have an admirer too? [*She takes the letter.*] Perhaps some one has read my book and liked it.

CHARLOTTE. And why shouldn't they? [*She is opening other letters.*]

ANNE. [*With a wistful smile as she looks at the table.*] Quite different from our little book of poems. . . .

CHARLOTTE. [*Smiling.*] Quite.

ANNE. And yet, I believe I think more of that poor little collection than of all our novels put together.

CHARLOTTE. [*Tearing open another letter.*] Naturally . . . our first-born. It paved the way for all this. . . .

ANNE. What a forlorn career . . . one short review and but two copies sold. [*Keeps dusting.*]

EMILY [*Grimly.*] I told you so. . . . Those poems belonged to us . . . alone. [*Dusts piano.*]

CHARLOTTE. [*Triumphantly holding up a check she has just taken from a letter.*] But what do you say to this? Emily, Anne—two hundred pounds royalty for "Jane Eyre."

EMILY. Success! . . .

ANNE. You're famous, Charlotte . . . or had I better call you Currer now? [*Laughing.*] The successful young author, Currer Bell, Esquire. [*Curtsies. Then touching* CHARLOTTE's *hand, timidly.*] I'm happy for you, dear, you *wanted* it so.

CHARLOTTE. [*Looking toward* EMILY.] But just have patience . . . you and Emily will be recognized too.

ANNE. [*As* EMILY *does not speak.*] Emily doesn't care. . . . She'd rather have it as it is, I'm sure. . . . And I . . . Well, what is to be will be. [*She hastily picks up a paper.*]

[EMILY *dusts back of chair behind table.*]

CHARLOTTE. Here's the "Quarterly Review." [*She opens it and finding the desired review, glances through it quickly. She chuckles.*] Hummm . . . *This* reviewer says here, with all the confidence in the world, that our three novels were written by *one* author named Currer Bell.

ANNE. I can understand how he would think that, can't you, Emily? Currer Bell is the successful one.

CHARLOTTE. But how stupid! Each novel is so different

. . . different in style, in characterization, in *every-thing!* You'd surely think "Wuthering Heights" was written by a virile Yorkshire man.

EMILY. [*Turning like a flash.*] Because it's coarse and brutal? [*Then as though to herself, with a grim smile.*] Eh?

ANNE. [*Hurrying to prevent a quarrel.*] I said from the beginning . . . Branwell might have written it.

CHARLOTTE. I'm sure he inspired it.

ANNE. Yes, for underneath all its brutality is a great *pity.*

EMILY. [*Scornfully.*] Pity!

ANNE. Yes, pity, Emily. You bring your lovers together again . . . even after death.

[EMILY *is at center right of table behind it, dusting.*]

CHARLOTTE. Let her deny that! [*There is a pause.*] But this is absurd . . . your novel could only be written by you . . . and I think the same can be said of mine and Anne's. This wretched reviewer has no discernment. [*She throws down the paper.*]

ANNE. Certainly the faults in mine are all my own.

[*While* ANNE *is speaking,* CHARLOTTE *unwraps a package and takes out a book.*]

CHARLOTTE. Look, Emily. . . . Look, Anne . . . the second edition of "Jane Eyre"!

ANNE. Oh . . . What lovely binding!

EMILY. [*Returning to the table.*] Plain Jane Eyre becoming beautiful! [*She squeezes* CHARLOTTE'S *hand.*] Well done! [*Turns to window.*]

CHARLOTTE. [*Flipping the pages.*] The print is excellent.

REV. BRONTË. [*Off stage.*] Charlotte! Charlotte!

CHARLOTTE. [*She abruptly tosses her head.*] I'm going to tell Papa!

ANNE. [*Startled.*] What? . . . Oh, about our writing, you mean?

CHARLOTTE. Yes.

EMILY. [*Through tight lips.*] You promised . . .

CHARLOTTE. That was about our book of poems. This is different.

EMILY. You promised.

CHARLOTTE. Papa's been puzzled for a long time about all the letters for Currer, Ellis and Acton Bell, and he'll wonder now where the money is coming from. Besides, I think he'll be happy to hear it . . . don't you think so?

ANNE. [*Glancing at* EMILY.] Y . . . yes. . . .

EMILY. Tell him only about "Jane Eyre" . . . your book . . . the success.

ANNE. Leave me out of it too.

EMILY. And of course, you'll warn him to keep the secret from Branwell. . . .

CHARLOTTE. Of course. . . .

[REV. BRONTË *comes from his study across the hall and calls as he shuffles toward the sitting-room door.*]

REV. BRONTË. Charlotte . . . Charlotte. . . .

CHARLOTTE. Yes, Papa?

[EMILY *exits to kitchen.* REV. BRONTË *enters the sitting-room.*]

REV. BRONTË. Did the papers come yet, Charlotte?

CHARLOTTE. Yes, Papa . . . they're all here. Which ones do you want? Shall I read to you this morning?

REV. BRONTË. No. . . . I can read the papers. . . . Every day since the operation I'm seeing better and feeling better, praise the good God. I only wish the same could be said for your brother. [*Peering through his spectacles at the stacks of papers and letters on the table.*] My, my, my . . . all that came this morning? . . . [EMILY *enters from kitchen.*] . . . *More* letters for the Bells? Come, come, Charlotte, this is too much. What is it all about?

CHARLOTTE. [*With a quick glance at her sisters.*] Papa . . . I've been writing a book.

REV. BRONTË. [*Calmly.*] Have you, my dear?

CHARLOTTE. Yes; and I want you to read it.

REV. BRONTË. [*Shaking his head.*] I'm afraid it will try my eyes too much . . . you write such a tiny hand, my dear.

CHARLOTTE. But it's not in manuscript; it's printed.

[*She hands a copy of the first volume of the second edition to her father.*]

REV. BRONTË. [*Squinting at it.*] But, my dear Charlotte . . . you've never thought of the expenses! It will be almost sure to be a loss. How can you get a book sold? No one knows you or your name.

CHARLOTTE. [*Smiling.*] Perhaps not my name . . . but maybe they know the name of Currer Bell.

REV. BRONTË. [*Stroking his chin.*] Currer Bell. . . . Hummm . . . so that's it? [*Smiling.*] *You're* . . .

CHARLOTTE. [*Smiling back at him.*] Currer Bell, *Esquire.* And I don't think the book will be a loss, Papa . . . that's the second edition, and the reviews have been splendid. [*Hands him book.*]

REV. BRONTË. [*Astonished.*] Reviews? Have there been any?

CHARLOTTE. [*Snatching up a sheaf of reviews from the drawer of the secretary.*] Oh, yes . . . many of them. [*Shoving them into his hand.*] Read them at your leisure, Papa.

REV. BRONTË. [*Shaking his head.*] Hmmm . . . well, well. Charlotte . . . well, well, daughter . . . reviews . . . hum. . . .

ANNE. Aren't you proud of our Charlotte, Papa?

REV. BRONTË. [*After a pause.*] Yes . . . but it's no more than I expected of her, Anne. Is she not my daughter? All of my children have my talent . . . my genius.

ANNE and CHARLOTTE. [*Together.*] We owe everything to you, Papa.

REV. BRONTË. [*Quick and startled.*] Does my poor son know of this?

EMILY. No, and you mustn't tell him.

CHARLOTTE. We must wait until he's better.

REV. BRONTË. [*Nodding slowly.*] I understand . . . yes, that is best. . . . But Branwell is the real genius, don't forget that. No matter what you do, Charlotte . . . or Anne . . . or any of us, he remains the genius. Just wait until he gets himself in hand . . . and he'll astonish the world.

ANNE. I'm sure he will, Papa.

CHARLOTTE. We know that, Papa . . . and that's why we're working so hard to help him. Today I received two hundred pounds in royalties.

REV. BRONTË. Two hundred pounds? My, my, Charlotte, you *are* a success.

CHARLOTTE. And there'll be much more later on.

REV. BRONTË. Really, my dear?

ANNE. Isn't it wonderful?

CHARLOTTE. Now we can easily send Branwell away to study.

REV. BRONTË. Eh? . . . Send him away? . . . to study. . . . Oh, yes, yes, to be sure . . . but not yet. . . . I can't let him go yet. . . . He's not strong enough.

CHARLOTTE. No, not yet, Papa, but as soon as he's able.

REV. BRONTË. [*Brushing aside his moment of fear.*] He'll get himself in hand, don't you worry. This is just the darker side of genius speaking in him.

ANNE. We understand that, Papa.

[EMILY *is calmly sewing. Sitting on stool near couch.*]

REV. BRONTË. He must plunge into hell to attain his heaven. Look at Lord Byron . . . and look at me . . . you girls have seen me drinking deep of dark waters, and your poor mother saw much more . . . much, much more. . . . [*Sighing.*]

CHARLOTTE. Don't condemn yourself, Papa.

REV. BRONTË. I fear I was unkind to her, at times. But could I help it? No! Something came upon me suddenly, seizing me with violence. I would go half mad. The blood would seem to explode in my veins. Red spots danced in my eyes. The world would be blotted out. Visions came to me then . . . some sublime, some most terrifying . . . but, remember this, Charlotte, it was while I struggled in one of those dark ways of passion I was inspired to write my profound poem, "The Vision of Hell." [*Pointing a shaking finger at Charlotte.*]

A great poem that, daughter . . . a great poem, by the Grace of God! Not yet recognized in this world of blind fools . . . [*Starts coughing.*] but nevertheless . . . [*His voice cracks and he is seized by a convulsive fit of coughing.*]

ANNE. [*Frightened.*] Shall I get you a cup of water, Papa?

[EMILY *goes at once to the crock of water she has left near the plant on the sill.*]

REV. BRONTË. [*Catching his breath.*] No . . . no . . . it will pass. . . . [*He coughs again, loudly, doubling up.*]

EMILY. [*Coming to him.*] Here, Papa . . . drink this.

REV. BRONTË. It's . . . it's nothing. . . .

EMILY. Drink it. . . .

[*She holds the crock to his mouth and he drinks, slobbering the water down his coat . . . it stops his coughing.*]

REV. BRONTË. [*Gasping.*] Ah . . . ah . . . thank you, Emily . . . thank you. . . .

EMILY. Another swallow?

ANNE. Take nine swallows, Papa.

EMILY. That's only for hiccoughs.

REV. BRONTË. That's . . . that's enough . . . I'm all right. . . . I'll go do some work on my sermon. . . . [*Shuffling to the door.*] And . . . and I'll read these,

Charlotte. . . . [*He holds up book and reviews: then shakes them at her, playfully.*] You . . . you . . . Currer Bell, *Esquire.* . . . I'm sure the book is much better than likely. [*He crosses the hall and exits into his study.*]

[EMILY *puts work basket from sofa on mantel.*]

CHARLOTTE. [*She and* ANNE *laughing merrily.*] He seems very pleased. I'm glad I told him. [*She goes back to the table where* EMILY *has put down the crock and is looking at the names on some of the letters.*] What are you looking for, Emily?

EMILY. I was looking to see if there was anything here for Branwell.

CHARLOTTE. I shouldn't think there would be. No one writes to Branwell any more. [*With a touch of scorn.*] Not even that terrible woman.

ANNE. I don't believe she ever did write to him, after he came home.

CHARLOTTE. I believe he wrote some of those letters to himself.

ANNE. He *did.* I saw his own handwriting on an envelope that was supposed to come from Thorp Green. . . .

EMILY. [*Accusingly.*] Anne. . . .

ANNE. [*Confused.*] I . . . I'm sorry, Emily.

CHARLOTTE. [*Again looking at her check.*] We'll send him away . . . to a place by the sea. . . .

EMILY. [*Still in a level unruffled tone.*] He doesn't want to go away now.

ANNE. Oh, not right now, of course.

CHARLOTTE. But as soon as possible.

EMILY. Not right now . . . or ever. All he wants money for is drink and opium.

CHARLOTTE. [*Tight-lipped, holding the check instinctively against her.*] He'll not get one twopence of *my* money for that.

EMILY. It's his only happiness.

CHARLOTTE. Happiness? Debauchery! He's a lost soul.

[BRANWELL *starts to descend stairs.*]

ANNE. [*Snatching at hope.*] Papa thinks he'll still find himself.

CHARLOTTE. We all know that's impossible now.

ANNE. Surely God could work a miracle.

EMILY. Your God is a stern and cruel God, Anne. He has no compassion for those who go exploring Hell.

[BRANWELL *is now in doorway. He has not shaved for a good many days and his tawny hair is uneven and long. His complexion is a waxy gray, and his body seems to have shrunk. He looks infinitely older than his thirty-one years. He is dressed carelessly in old trousers and shirt, open at the throat, over which he has flung a rather dirty and crumpled dressing-gown. In the pockets of the gown are letters and papers which bulge and protrude.*]

ANNE. [*Frightened.*] We must not give up hope.

CHARLOTTE. [*Sorting the mail on table.*] We're not, dear. We couldn't go on living if we gave up hope.

[BRANWELL *in doorway.*]

EMILY. [*Seeing* BRANWELL. *Quickly.*] Branwell. . . .

CHARLOTTE. [*Swiftly gathers letters and papers to her bosom.*] How are you feeling, Branwell?

[BRANWELL *crosses to her and gazes intently into her eyes. He runs his fingers over the letters she holds and snatches one. Crosses behind her to the lower window.*]

BRANWELL. [*Looking at the letter—reading the name on the envelope.*] Currer Bell— [*Then he tears up the letter and holds the scraps in his hand.*]

CHARLOTTE. [*Breathlessly to* EMILY.] He should go back to bed, he's too weak to stay up. . . .

ANNE. [*To* EMILY.] Don't let him go out of doors, that autumn wind is very cold.

[ANNE *and* CHARLOTTE *exit quickly into kitchen.* BRANWELL *turns from window and moodily crosses up toward center door.*]

EMILY. [*As* BRANWELL *stands undecided, looking at the front door.*] Branwell . . . where are you going? [*He looks at her but doesn't reply.*] Come in here . . . by the fire . . . where it's warm.

BRANWELL. No . . . I think . . . I think I'll . . . I'll . . .

EMILY. [*Leading him down.*] Yes, come here and talk to me. [*He turns, comes to her.*] You haven't talked to any of us for such a long time. [*After another pause,* BRANWELL *comes back into room—he looks away from* EMILY, *but she turns his face to hers with gentle hands.*] I thought I left you asleep.

BRANWELL. [*His long, bony fingers plucking at the hem of his dressing-robe.*] I was . . . I was asleep . . . I think . . . but something like a stone fell on my chest and woke me up. It was like a gravestone . . . falling on my chest . . . crushing it. Then there was pain . . . dull pain . . . here. [*He touches his heart and coughs.*]

EMILY. Come here . . . by the fire.

[*She gives him her wiry arm to lean on. He crosses the room, clinging to her.*]

BRANWELL. Good old girl. . . . [*He drops into a chair.*] Wish I had your strength.

EMILY. You'll get your strength again . . . don't worry. I'll poke up the fire. [*She stoops in front of the grate and pokes the coals into a blaze.*]

BRANWELL. What . . . what happened to *me*, Emily? [*She looks at him, as the scraps of the Currer Bell letter drop from his hand.*] I had *everything* once. I could have done things. . . . I *wanted* to do things . . . and then . . . then what happened? What happened do you suppose? When did it all begin?

EMILY. I don't know what you mean. [*Her back is*

turned to him as she still squats and pokes viciously at the fire.]

BRANWELL. Oh, yes you do, old girl . . . *you* understand. Nobody else does, but *you* do. [EMILY *turns to him.*] Something went wrong all of a sudden, inside of me. I wish I knew when . . . if I could just put my finger on it.

EMILY. What good would that do you? Don't talk . . . you'll get to coughing.

BRANWELL. Perhaps it began when I was lost on the moors. Remember, Emily? You girls ran away and left me up by the falls near Penistone. Suddenly I was all alone . . . under that vast sky . . . a little mite . . . alone with the black stones and the wind crying in the heather. I can remember to this day the fear I felt . . . how I tried to scream and couldn't make a sound. I can see myself running . . . running like a wild thing through the heather, and the big grouse starting up before me, whirring their wings and screaming . . . screaming the way I wanted to scream. I never liked the moors since then, and I never wanted to stay alone. I had to have people around me . . . many people . . . jolly people . . . and warmth and cheer . . . nothing gray or lonely. Perhaps it began then, Emily . . . do you think?

EMILY. [*Touches him with a gesture of understanding.*] Perhaps. . . .

BRANWELL. [*Slumping down on the couch.*] It . . . began and I couldn't stop it. It ate me . . . inside . . .

like a worm. It ate my heart . . . and my courage . . .
and my ambition. It got fat on my ambition. . . . It
ate it all up, every morsel of it . . . and now . . .
now I'm a failure . . . a rotten, mean little failure.
. . . [*He breaks down, burying his face in his hands,
moaning.*]

EMILY. [*Leaping up. Quickly seizing his head between
her hands, covering his mouth.*] Stop, Branwell! Stop!
Stop! [*The harshness of her tone startles him. He sobs
through her lines.*] Don't show it to me! Keep it
covered up. It's not a nice thing to look at.

BRANWELL. I'm . . . I'm sorry, old girl . . . sorry.
[*He rises wearily and crosses to window—looking out.*]
I . . . I didn't want to go to my grave unsung . . .
obscure . . . a nobody. I wanted to join the Immortals,
Emily . . . one of that brave company. . . . I *could*
have . . . it was my heritage . . . but I threw it away.
. . . It's too late now . . . too late for me.

EMILY. [*Quietly.*] Perhaps not too late. Strange things
can happen to you, for you are moor born, Branwell.
[BRANWELL *looks at* EMILY.] Yes . . . moor born
. . . and what the moors took from you, they may return.

BRANWELL. [*Shaking his head, loosely.*] No . . . no
. . . I'm stripped down to the bone . . . I'm naked
and cold. . . . [*He digs into a pocket of his dressing-
gown and pulls out a handful of crumpled, much-read
letters. A few of them scatter to the floor. Abruptly.*]
Emily. . . .

EMILY. Yes, Branwell?

BRANWELL. [*He comes quickly down to her. Fingering the letters.*] Did I show you the last letter she wrote me?

EMILY. Yes, Branwell. . . .

BRANWELL. I don't think you saw the *last* one . . . it came only a week ago.

EMILY. You've lost count. It was much longer than that.

BRANWELL. How long?

EMILY. Oh . . . months, anyway.

BRANWELL. [*Shaking his head.*] Hummmmm . . . months . . . years. . . . Look here, Emily, that's her husband's fault. . . . He made a will . . . it said she wouldn't get a shilling if she married me.

EMILY. You don't know whether that's true or not.

BRANWELL. [*Excited.*] I do! I do! He went to his grave with bitterness in his heart. . . . *I'd* be afraid to go to my grave like that. . . .

EMILY. Why don't you burn these letters, Branwell?

[*She puts letters behind her.*]

BRANWELL. [*Half leaping up from his chair.*] No . . . no . . . give them to me . . . they're all I have . . . give them to me. . . . [*He takes letters forcibly from* EMILY.]

EMILY. [*As she lets him take them.*] *She* has forgotten. Why don't you?

BRANWELL. [*Proudly.*] I'm not that kind. . . . I love . . . to the grave . . . and beyond the grave. . . . [*He stuffs the letters back into the pocket of his gown.*] Don't suggest such things. . . . [*Half sobbing.*] Don't suggest such things. . . .

EMILY. [*Quietly.*] Very well . . . don't take on so. I only thought sometimes it's good to rid yourself of things that bind you to a past that's dead.

BRANWELL. [*With a low moan.*] Oh . . . that pain again . . . over my heart . . . around my heart. . . . [*He lurches down on couch.*] I . . . I can't stand it, Emily . . . I must have relief . . . I must . . . I must. . . . [*Clasping his hands fiercely together— then seizing her as she stands above him.*] Help me, Emily . . . [*Clutches at her.*] . . . help me. . . . [*Whimpering.*] Help me . . . for God's sake.

EMILY. What do you want me to do?

BRANWELL. Get me out of this prison-house . . . away from these choking tombstones . . . stop that damned wind from blowing . . . if you love me, stop it. . . . I'm lonely . . . I'm afraid. . . .

EMILY. No, not *afraid,* Branwell!

BRANWELL. Yes . . . yes . . . afraid. . . . Help me to forget, Emily. . . . Let me go where it's warm . . . where I can talk with men . . . where I can drown myself . . . destroy my senses. I don't want to think any more.

EMILY. Be quiet, Branwell. You mean you want to go to the Black Bull tavern?

BRANWELL. Yes . . . yes . . . it's warm there. . . . I have friends there . . . friends who understand me. It's not lonely and cold . . . but . . . but I can't go unless I have some money . . . a crown . . . two crowns, that's all. Only one, if you can't spare more. They won't let me drink without money, or get that other thing. . . . [*Winking craftily.*] You know . . . you know, Emily.

EMILY. [*After a quick glance toward the hall door.*] You may go to the tavern . . . if it will make you happy. [*She crosses to the left side of the table, opens her desk which rests upon it, and takes out a small purse, from which she extracts three coins—English crowns.*] Here are three crowns.

BRANWELL. [*Snatching them.*] Oh, Emily . . . you're fine . . . you understand me . . . you're not a prig like Charlotte . . . or afraid like little Anne. . . . [*He is struggling out of his dressing-gown.*] I'll . . . I'll pay this back. . . . Oh, yes, I . . . I always pay my debts. . . . [*He throws the dressing-gown into a chair.*] God bless you, for a hearty fellow, Emily. . . . [*He starts to doorway quickly.*]

EMILY. Are you going like that? Get your coat.

BRANWELL. I'm quite all right . . . it's only a little way.

EMILY. But the wind's cold, blowing over the moor-crest.

BRANWELL. I won't know it blows in the tavern . . .
warm there . . . only a little way to go . . . I'll
run. . . . God bless you, Emily.

[*He stops abruptly and dashes back to where she stands,
below table. He throws his arms violently about her, and
kisses her savagely on the face and neck.* EMILY *pushes
him away.* BRANWELL *exits running.*]

EMILY. Go . . . go. . . . Quiet, they'll stop you if
they hear you. . . .

[*For a moment* EMILY *stands motionless, rigid. She
turns and crosses to door. Abruptly turns; takes a
nervous step or two toward piano, then sits quickly on
piano stool and almost in a frenzy she strikes the keys
in the opening bars of a classic composition.*]

CURTAIN

PART FOUR

Night of same day.
Wind. Moonlight through the windows. REV.
BRONTË'S *voice is heard from up stairway.*

REV. BRONTË. Branwell. . . . Branwell. . . .

[CHARLOTTE *enters from kitchen carrying lamp. Puts
it on table.*]

REV. BRONTË. Emily—Charlotte—is Branwell home yet?

CHARLOTTE. No, Papa. [*To herself.*] And it's turned
so cold. He went without his coat. . . . Oh dear, it
will be the death of him. [ANNE *enters hurriedly.*]
Anne, did you find him?

ANNE. No. Who could have given him the money?

CHARLOTTE. You're sure he had some?

ANNE. Yes. They told me so at the tavern. About three
crowns, and after he'd spent it all, they said he rode
away in a gig with some drunken companion.

CHARLOTTE. Those dissolute friends of his . . .
Brown. What about him?

ANNE. Brown was at the tavern when I went in. He
swore he knew nothing about it.

CHARLOTTE. A likely story! [*Then after a pause . . .*

thoughtfully.] It just occurred to me . . . *Emily* might have given it to him.

ANNE. Emily? Oh, she wouldn't . . . *not* Emily, she loves him so much.

CHARLOTTE. When we love some one, aren't we quite often too indulgent?

ANNE. Yes, but . . . but that would be too *cruel*. For over a week now he hasn't had a thing to drink, and it seemed to me he was calmer . . . more peaceful. *Now* we'll have to begin all over again. [*She turns back to the window anxiously.*]

[*The voice of the wind increases.*]

ANNE. [*After a pause.*] Winter's beginning early . . . the heather's dead already . . . and the birds have gone.

CHARLOTTE. You dread it, don't you, Anne?

ANNE. I don't seem to stand it as well as I used to.

CHARLOTTE. Never mind . . . success is here. We'll go away from Haworth.

ANNE. [*Shaking her head.*] Do you think so? Haworth holds us fast.

CHARLOTTE. We'll break away. How would you like to spend some time in poor Auntie's country, Penzance? . . . warm, flowery Penzance. . . . Do you remember how she always talked about it?

ANNE. Yes . . . poor Auntie . . . a little lady from

Penzance, imprisoned in Yorkshire. I don't believe she ever got the chill out of her bones.

CHARLOTTE. Would you like to go there, Anne?

ANNE. I should like it, I think . . . but I can wait . . . don't worry about *me*.

CHARLOTTE. Well, we shall see. . . .

[*Another pause.*]

REV. BRONTË. [*Entering from his study. He is in a state of extreme agitation. His clothing is disarranged and his features distorted.*] Charlotte! Charlotte!

CHARLOTTE. [*Rising.*] Yes . . . Papa?

REV. BRONTË. [*Entering the sitting-room.*] Has . . . has he come back yet?

CHARLOTTE. No, Papa.

REV. BRONTË. Then I'm going after him.

CHARLOTTE. [*Going to him.*] What good will that do? He's not at the tavern.

REV. BRONTË. He might be.

ANNE. No, Papa. I told you I just returned from there. They said he went off in a gig, at least two hours ago.

REV. BRONTË. But *I* can find him . . . I'll call him. . . . He'll answer his father.

CHARLOTTE. [*Holding him by the arm.*] *Please,* Papa . . . it's so cold out . . . you're not strong.

REV. BRONTË. [*Throwing off* CHARLOTTE'S *restraining arm.*] Do you realize what's happening? Your brother is out there in the cold and wind . . . it might be the end of him. . . . [EMILY *enters hallway from left.*] Suppose he should die through our carelessness? Think how terrible that would be . . . cut down in his prime . . . before he realizes his great promise. Did you think of that, Charlotte?

[CHARLOTTE *starts to speak.*]

REV. BRONTË. No, you didn't think of it . . . you're selfish. . . . A genius is in your keeping and you think only of yourself . . . of your own success! I'm going to find my son.

EMILY. [*Appearing in the doorway. She is as calm as a stone.*] What's the matter, Papa?

REV. BRONTË. [*Going to her.*] Emily . . . Emily, your brother is out there . . . dying perhaps . . . and we stay here, doing nothing. I'm going after him.

EMILY. That will do no good. Let him alone. He'll come back. He's come back before.

REV. BRONTË. You too, Emily? . . . [*Throws her off.*] You too . . . turning against him? He thinks more of you than any of us. . . . Oh, yes . . . yes he does. He told me so. . . . You've always helped him. . . . You must help him *now!*

EMILY. I'll do all I can . . . but there's no use going after him. Who knows where he is?

REV. BRONTË. That's just it . . . who knows? Who cares? [*Strikes table with cane.*] Perhaps he's wandering on the moors . . . alone.

EMILY. [*Shaking her head.*] No . . . not on the moors. He'll stay away from the moors. [*Crossing toward the fire.*] It's more likely he's in some warm chimney nook, singing his songs . . . telling his stories . . . drowning himself.

REV. BRONTË. [*Staring at her.*] Drowning himself? Don't say that! That's just what I'm afraid of, Emily . . . afraid he'll destroy himself. He's threatened to blow out his brains with my pistols. I've had to hide them lately.

EMILY. I didn't mean that . . . but don't be afraid. *He* won't destroy himself.

REV. BRONTE. You don't know. In the depths of his despair he might do anything.

EMILY. Anything . . . but that.

[*Suddenly a dog begins to bark, indistinctly, in the wind. The four people in the room stop still and listen.*]

ANNE. That's Keeper barking. [*She goes down to the front window.*]

CHARLOTTE. It's . . . perhaps . . . [*The dog continues to bark, fiercely.*] some strangers. . . . [CHARLOTTE *crosses to* ANNE *at window.*]

REV. BRONTË. [*Fearfully.*] Strangers? . . . At this

time of night? Oh my God. They're bringing bad news.
[*He shakes from head to foot.*]

ANNE [*Peering through the window.*] There're two
people coming up the path. . . . One is . . . Oh, it's
Branwell with . . . with . . .

REV. BRONTË. Branwell . . . Branwell . . .

EMILY. [*Snatches lamp from table.*] Wait, Papa. [*She
goes into hall. Puts lamp on stairs. Opens outer door.*]

REV. BRONTË. Oh, Branwell, my son . . . my son. . . .

[BRANWELL *and* CHRISTOPHER, *a rugged, Yorkshire
farmhand, are heard as they enter in outer hallway.*]

BRANWELL. Brown thought the story was funny . . .
but he didn't laugh. My voice was good tonight . . .
hi . . . not so fast, my hearty. [*They appear in center
doorway.*] Did I tell you? Cressman's daughter had a
child by me. But it was born as still as a stone.

EMILY. In here.

BRANWELL. [*As he is being put in chair back of table
by* EMILY *and* CHRISTOPHER.] Thanks . . . thanks,
old codger . . . good Samaritan. . . .

REV. BRONTË. [*Furiously, crosses to right of* CHRIS-
TOPHER. *Shaking him.*] You . . . you drunken lout
. . . you . . . you devil. Look what you've done to
my son.

CHRISTOPHER. Ee—don't be blamin' me, yer Reverence,
don't be blamin' me. I ain't ta blame fer it. I never

seed 'im this evenin' till I eered 'im, talkin' an singin'
to 'issel' int ditch.

REV. BRONTË. [*Crosses to chair right of table. Sits.*]
Branwell—Branwell. . . .

BRANWELL. Sorry you had to disturb me . . . of
course you didn't know . . . how could you? But just
when you shook me, there was a great poem a-borning
in me . . . a great poem with music, sweeping in on
me from the moors . . . sweeping in . . . on the back
of the wind. I don't blame you . . . but I lost it . . .
lost it. . . .

REV. BRONTË. Branwell, look at your father.

CHRISTOPHER. Ee seemed right 'appy enuff. First I was
a mand to let 'im be. But then there war a queer
rattlin' come int 'is throat when 'e stopped singin' like
'e couldna be breathin' proper, so I manded to be
bringin' 'im hame ter ye.

CHARLOTTE. That's kind of you.

CHRISTOPHER. Ee—that's all right, Miss. An' nar I'll
be ganging.

CHARLOTTE. You're Christopher Sythe of Fanstone
Manor, aren't you?

CHRISTOPHER. Ay, Miss Brontë.

CHARLOTTE. I thought I recognized your face. My sister
and I came to visit your wife when she was sick, some
months ago.

CHRISTOPHER. Ay, Miss Brontë, an' reet kind o' ye it
war.

CHARLOTTE. I know you'll not speak of this to any one, will you, Christopher?

CHRISTOPHER. Ee not me, Miss Brontë. Cut out me tongue wi' a sickle iffen I breathes as much as a word ont.

[*As* CHARLOTTE *leads* CHRISTOPHER *out,* CHRISTOPHER *and* BRANWELL *speak together.*]

CHRISTOPHER	BRANWELL
An' nar excusin' mesel' I'll gang along. It's a dark night an' a long ways to Fanstone Manor an' jobs fer Maister Fanstone when I gets there. G'night, Miss Brontë.	Tell him not to go. Don't go yet, old friend. Don't go. I want to talk to you. Pull up a chair by the fire. Tell him not to go, Emily.

[*Door slam and wind on* CHRISTOPHER'S *exit.*]

REV. BRONTË. Hush, he must.

BRANWELL. [*Snuggling close to* EMILY'S *breast as she continues to support him, her body erect.*] Fine fellow that . . . noble fellow . . . only he shouldn't have disturbed me, Emily. . . . I tell you, it was a mighty poem a-borning in me. . . .

EMILY. Yes, Branwell. . . .

ANNE. [*To* EMILY.] Let's take him upstairs.

BRANWELL. [*Unheeding.*] And then . . . then he shouted at me . . . and shook me . . . and I lost it . . . it went away on the wind . . . back to the moors.

. . . It came from the moors, Emily. . . . Strange, wasn't it? . . . But I'll never find it again.

EMILY. Yes, you will, Branwell.

BRANWELL. [*He shakes his head; then laughs, softly.*] I don't care . . . I'm happy . . . and warm, Emily, old girl . . . quite warm . . . [*A peculiar rattling comes into his throat.*] . . . warm and tired.

EMILY. Yes . . . you'll sleep now.

BRANWELL. Sleep . . . without a dream. . . .

REV. BRONTË. [*Touching him.*] Branwell . . . it's your father, Branwell. . . . Come up to bed. I'll take care of you. Branwell, won't you look at me?

BRANWELL. [*Turning to his father. He puts hand on* REV. BRONTË'S *hand which is supported by cane.*] Sorry, old man . . . I *have* made a mess of it for you, haven't I? [*His voice trails away. The rattling in his throat comes again.*]

ANNE. [*Frightened.*] Father . . . pray for him!

[*Without a word,* REV. BRONTË *sinks to his old knees, clasps his hands and begins to mumble a prayer.*]

BRANWELL. I tell you, Emily, it was a great poem a-borning in me—

EMILY. Yes, Branwell, darling.

BRANWELL. Warm . . . thanks to you, Emily. . . . Those three crowns you gave me. . . .

CHARLOTTE. [*Horrified.*] Emily! . . . You *did* give it to him—

EMILY. [*Going on, as though* CHARLOTTE *has not spoken.*] Come, Branwell . . . you must lie down now.

BRANWELL. [*Feebly.*] N . . . no . . . no. . . . I'm happy here with you. . . . [REV. BRONTË *starts to pray silently.* BRANWELL *moans softly, pressing both hands to his heart.*] That pain . . . soft pain. . . .

REV. BRONTË. Take him not from me, Lord God. . . .

BRANWELL. I want . . . Oh, Emily, *you* know . . .

[*He slumps on table.*]

REV. BRONTË. Almighty God, take him not from me. . . . He has yet great works to do.

[EMILY *has succeeded in getting* BRANWELL *to his feet.*]

BRANWELL. Amen to that, old man! [*He crumples and sinks nearly to the floor behind the table.* EMILY *holds him.* BRANWELL *looks up at* EMILY *and gasps, an expression of fear and horror on his face.*] Emily—Emily— [*His head falls forward.*]

EMILY. [*Dragging him to his feet.*] Not on your knees, Branwell . . . not on your knees. . . . Stand up to it, Branwell! Stand up to it!

[BRANWELL *makes a supreme effort; lifts his head, stands straight, and supported by* EMILY'S *arm, he dies, without another word or sound. His face is calm and childlike. His open eyes are mild.*]

CHARLOTTE. Emily held him up . . . to die.

REV. BRONTË. [*Still praying fiercely, swaying on his knees.*] Don't take him from me, my Heavenly Father . . . don't take him from me!

THE CURTAIN FALLS

PART FIVE

Three months later. The parsonage sitting-room. About noon. Winter is in Yorkshire but the heavy snows are yet to come.
Rise on empty stage.
MARTHA *enters from stairs at rise, running. She is very much excited and flushed, and she comes straight to the sitting-room.*

MARTHA. [*As she comes downstairs.*] Oh, Miss Anne . . . Miss Anne. . . . [ANNE *enters from kitchen right.*] Miss Emily's gettin' up.

ANNE. Oh, she mustn't do that!

MARTHA. I tol' her she ought not to be doin' it, but you know Miss Emily . . . [*Shrugging.*] . . . not a muckle o' use sayin' Nay to the likes o' her.

ANNE. [*Snatching at any ray of hope.*] Perhaps it's because she's feeling much better?

MARTHA. Sorry, but I dunna think that's it. She kin hardly set up, she's that weak, an' her breathin's fearsome loud an' thick-like. Would *you* care to be a-speakin' to her, Miss Anne?

ANNE. [*Looking at* MARTHA *sorrowfully.*] You know I'm as helpless as you are, Martha, or any of us, if she's set her mind on it. [*Up to door.*]

MARTHA. She says as how she'll be comin' down here.

ANNE. Oh . . . well, maybe the change will do her good. [*Crossing the room.*] I'll poke up the fire, it'll be more cheerful.

MARTHA. Looks to me like Miss Emily wants to die . . . yesterday mornin' I went up to bring her some tea, and there I found 'er up fraim 'er bed . . . standin' in the open window, dressed only in her night gown, a-lettin' the cald wind blow over 'er fram t'moors. . . . Ah, it war daft o' 'er. I shut the window quick an' made 'er get 'ersel' back t' bed . . . but I dare say she got up, soon as I left, and opened it again.

ANNE. [*At fireplace.*] And the way she behaved at Branwell's funeral. . . . [EMILY *starts down staircase slowly.*] She wouldn't wear a cloak and she stood in the gateway, letting the rain pour down on her bare head . . . her skirts were clinging to her when she stood by the grave. . . .

MARTHA. Ay, an' not one o' us could be makin' 'er change um . . . fra hours afterwards. . . .

ANNE. [*Starting up. Looks toward stairs.*] Sh-h-h she's coming down. [ANNE *crosses up to center doorway.*]

MARTHA. [*Crosses to doorway, looks up then crosses to behind sofa.*] Poor lass . . . she used to take those steps like any mon.

[EMILY *enters painfully, slowly, in nightdress. . . . She carries comb and her note-book.*]

ANNE. Emily, dear . . . you shouldn't have come down.

EMILY. I . . . I wanted to see you. . . .

ANNE. I could have come up there. . . . [*Attempts to support* EMILY.]

EMILY. Don't help me, ninny. . . .

ANNE. But, Emily . . .

EMILY. I can walk alone . . . you see . . . quite well. [*She crosses unsteadily over to fireplace.*]

[TABBY *enters from kitchen.*]

MARTHA. [*To* ANNE.] I'll . . . I'll fetch some warm milk for 'er. [*She crosses quickly toward kitchen and almost runs down* TABBY.]

TABBY. [*Fiercely.*] Wot's that stubborn un out o' 'er bed for?

MARTHA. Arsk 'er yer simpleton's questions yersel' . . . while I'm not wastin' time to be 'elpin' 'er.

[TABBY *crosses* MARTHA, *then* MARTHA *exits kitchen.*]

TABBY. [*To* ANNE *in lowered voice.*] Wot's she up to, tell me that?

ANNE. [*Quietly.*] She wants to be near the fire, Tabby, and wouldn't you if you were ill? It's not any too warm upstairs, or cheerful. . . .

TABBY. Humph. She's no business to be a-doin' it. You'd better be gettin' a doctor fer 'er right quick.

ANNE. You know she won't see one . . . and she re-

fuses to take a drop of that medicine Doctor Epps sent
us from London.

TABBY. I asks you, don't she want to get well. . . .
I asks you—don't she want to get well?

ANNE. I don't know, Tabby. . . . I don't know. She's
locked herself away from us, tighter than ever since
Branwell died. [EMILY *starts combing her hair. Standing at fireplace.*] Can't . . . can't I comb it for you,
Emily?

TABBY. It's like she went down in the grave to
him. . . . [*Mumbles, as she exits into kitchen.*] It
be the fairish got into you alone on the moors—
[*Exits.*]

ANNE. Please, Emily . . .

EMILY. No, no . . . no. First it's can you help me
walk . . . then can you comb my hair for me. . . .
[*She weakly combs hair as she crosses to chair right
of table.*] Look how strong she is . . . she combs . . .
her own hair. . . . [*Sits right of table.*]

ANNE. Of course I only thought . . .

EMILY. [*Smiles at* ANNE *reassuringly.*] Sit down, Anne.
[ANNE *crosses, caresses her and goes to window to her
embroidery frame.*] Where's Papa?

ANNE. Lying down in his study.

EMILY. The old tree is . . . struck. . . .

ANNE. Yes. Oh, Emily, I don't think he'll ever get over
Branwell's going. I was talking to him just before

breakfast . . . his faith in God seems to be sorely shaken. He can't believe that a just God could take Branwell away in a time of promise.

EMILY. He knows now how cruel God can be. . . .

ANNE. He says it's like blighting the wheat before the harvest.

EMILY. Charlotte sees only mercy in it. . . .

ANNE. Yes, yes . . . I see that too . . . but poor Branwell . . . he didn't think that way.

EMILY. No. [*Looks intently at her note-book.*] Where's Charlotte?

ANNE. Out for a moment.

EMILY. Anne—are you too afraid to make me a promise? I mean . . . a promise that you will always keep?

ANNE. If . . . if . . . I make you a promise . . . I will always keep it.

EMILY. Even when they *tear* at you?

ANNE. Tear at me? Oh what is it? Tell me. . . .

EMILY. I have written here. . . . [CHARLOTTE *enters the hallway.* EMILY *rises and crosses to sofa.*] Not now. . . .

CHARLOTTE. [*Calling in hallway.*] Anne. . . .

EMILY. [*Sits on sofa.*] Another . . . *better* time. . . . [*Resumes combing her hair.*]

ANNE. Yes, Charlotte. . . . [*Charlotte enters in bonnet and cloak.*] Oh, didn't you find any?

CHARLOTTE. Oh, Anne—only this . . . such a little withered bit. Do you think she'd like to see it . . . it might depress her. . . . Emily . . . you downstairs? You know you shouldn't do this. You must stay in your warm bed.

EMILY. [*Tugging at her hair.*] People only *die* in bed. . . .

CHARLOTTE. Emily, listen to me. I'm going to be really severe with you. . . .

EMILY. What now?

CHARLOTTE. No nonsense this time. I'm going to send for a doctor . . . you are going to see him today.

EMILY. Why should I?

CHARLOTTE. Because you're no better than you were yesterday . . . in fact your breathing sounds worse.

ANNE. Please see a doctor, Emily . . . if not for yourself, for us. We only want to see you get well.

EMILY. I am well. . . .

CHARLOTTE. Don't keep saying that. Why, you've no strength left . . . and only a short time ago you were stronger than any of us.

EMILY. I'm better, I tell you. Must I dance a jig to show you?

ANNE. Oh, Emily . . . is it really true?

EMILY. Yes.

CHARLOTTE. I don't believe it, Emily.

EMILY. Would you rather see me dying?

CHARLOTTE. [*Hurt.*] How can you speak that way? I meant . . . you're only saying that to keep from seeing a doctor.

EMILY. [*Grimly.*] Doctor? I want no poisoning doctors here.

CHARLOTTE. You see . . . another silly notion. What have you got against doctors?

EMILY. A witch with spells and potions would do as well.

CHARLOTTE. *Now* you're talking nonsense.

EMILY. Don't, Charlotte. I'm hardly fit to quarrel with you, now.

CHARLOTTE. [*Gently.*] We won't quarrel. We never really have. . . . I didn't mean— Look, Emily, what I found for you. [*Holds up sprig of heather.*]

EMILY. Yes? What is it?

CHARLOTTE. Don't you recognize your favorite flower? Heather. It is the only spray I could find.

EMILY. Heather? [*Slowly nodding.*] Oh yes, to be sure . . . dead, isn't it? The bloom all gone . . . bitten by the heavy frost and the ice in the wind. Poor . . . [*She coughs.*]

CHARLOTTE. I walked miles over the moors to find it for you, Emily. I had almost given up when suddenly I saw this.

EMILY. How was the day—out there?

CHARLOTTE. Cold. Desolate, Emily. Not a bird, no sound but the wind rattling the bare branches of the thorn.

EMILY. A good day for walking far. . . .

ANNE. Charlotte, shouldn't we make her stay in her warm bed?

CHARLOTTE. She's probably lonely up there and won't admit it.

ANNE. [*To divert* EMILY's *mind.*] Charlotte, a lot of new letters have just come.

CHARLOTTE. [*At table.*] Were there any reviews?

ANNE. I think so.

CHARLOTTE. Here's a letter from Mr. Thackeray.

ANNE. Mr. Thackeray, Emily.

CHARLOTTE. How famous we are!

ANNE. Oh yes, we are!

CHARLOTTE. Here's the "North American." There's something in this. Perhaps Emily would like to hear it.

ANNE. Would you, dear? Read it to us, Charlotte, let's hear some more about ourselves.

EMILY. Perhaps we can laugh.

CHARLOTTE. [*Who has found the review and is glancing through it.*] *This* might amuse you, Emily. Ellis Bell—here you are, it says "Ellis Bell is a man of uncommon talents—but dogged, brutal and morose. . . ." [*Then sadly as she looks at* EMILY.] I wish they could *see* you.

EMILY. [*Smiling, faintly.*] I think . . . it fits me perfectly. . . . [*But without real interest.*] What else . . . does it say? [*She drops her comb; reaches for it; has not the strength to get it again. She lets it lie on the hearth, close to the coals.*]

CHARLOTTE. [*Shaking her head.*] What a bad set the Bells must be! What appalling books they write! You're not alone, Emily . . . we're *all* in for it. A wicked lot!

[EMILY *tries to recover comb but is too weak.*]

ANNE. They turn on us now because they've discovered we are women.

EMILY. Anne . . . I dropped my comb. . . . I can't seem to . . . to . . . It may burn, so close to the fire. . . .

[ANNE *hurries over and lifts* EMILY *back to a comfortable position on sofa.*]

ANNE. Let me help you, dear, I'll get it for you. [*She crosses to fireplace and picks up comb.*] It was just about to burn. It's too hot to use now. [*She sets it on the stones, some distance from the grate.*] Shall I fetch another one for you?

EMILY. [*Lying back on the sofa, closing her eyes.*]
N . . . no . . . not now. . . .

CHARLOTTE. There's nothing they've left out. *My* book
bears the marks of more than one mind and one sex
. . . and yours, Emily . . . Oh, good heavens . . .
[*She tosses down the review.*] I'll not go on with it.
. . . Let's read something else.

EMILY. [*Opening her eyes.*] Read *that*, Charlotte.
[*With scorn.*] Am I afraid of anything *they* could say?

CHARLOTTE. But it's utter foolishness . . . not even
amusing.

EMILY. *I* might be amused by it. [*Moves to left end of
couch. Holding out an unsteady hand.*] Then give it to
me. . . . I'll read it.

CHARLOTTE. You're sure it won't upset you?

EMILY. [*Smiling, wanly.*] How little you know me,
Charlotte. [*She takes the paper.*]

CHARLOTTE. You won't *let* me know you . . . if you
only would. [*Closer to the sofa.*] Oh, Emily, we're together such a little while on earth. Let's not shut each
other out, to live in loneliness. We'll be so lonely in our
graves.

EMILY. [*Holding the paper in front of her face, and
speaking as though* CHARLOTTE *has not spoken.*] It's
dark in here.

ANNE. Too dark for you to read it, dear?

CHARLOTTE. I'll read it to you.

EMILY. No . . . there's more light now. For a moment the sun had gone behind a cloud. . . . [*She reads to herself.*]

[ANNE *and* CHARLOTTE *look at each other again. The light in the room had not changed.*]

EMILY. [*Reads from "North American Review."*] "The family mind is strikingly peculiar, giving a strong impression of unity—but it is still male and female—seems to have a sense of the depravity of human nature— The Bells have a brother—is it not possible that his masculine hand might have written 'Wuther—'" [*Putting down the magazine.*] So they could believe that, could they?

CHARLOTTE. [*Takes magazine from* EMILY.] I told you it was foolishness.

EMILY. [*Unheeding.*] Branwell . . . might have written it. . . .

CHARLOTTE. We'll never allow them to think that. They're not going to keep on saying that "Wuthering Heights" was written by Branwell or me or anybody else. Bitter or sweet, you must taste success.

ANNE. Don't upset her, Charlotte. If Emily wants obscurity don't force open the door. Remember her poem:

> "Oh for the time when I shall sleep
> Without identity
> And never care how rain may steep
> Or snow may cover me."

[EMILY *touches* ANNE *lovingly.*]

CHARLOTTE. But she's written a great book. It hasn't been recognized yet, but that doesn't make it any the less great. Branwell had a kind of talent which he dissipated. But Emily has genius. The world has to know about you. That's all.

EMILY. [*Her voice hoarse and her breathing still difficult.*] He lies obscure in his grave. . . . Do you understand, Charlotte? . . . Obscure . . . in his grave. . . .

CHARLOTTE. *We* remember him . . . and only with forgiveness and pity.

EMILY. [*Her lip curling.*] Pity! A poor recompense for all his yearning . . . for all his anguish. [*Looking at* CHARLOTTE *with dimming eyes.*] Why should I alone understand his cry for recognition? Surely *you* should.

CHARLOTTE. I do understand it . . . . but what belongs to you shall not be his.

EMILY. I don't want it. . . . Let it go to him. Perhaps in some strange way he'll know.

CHARLOTTE. No, Emily . . . that would be wrong!

EMILY. The gift is mine . . . to bestow on him. . . . [*As a blast of wintry moor wind strikes the house.*] What was that? [EMILY *starts up, almost frightened.*]

ANNE. Only the wind . . . your moor wind, pouring over the moor-crest, Emily. . . . How could *you* mistake it?

EMILY. [*Dropping back.*] There was . . . there was a voice in it . . . and at the window there was some one . . . some one scratching to get in . . . some one locked out, who doesn't like the loneliness . . . some coward soul, afraid of the moors. . . . [*Almost whispering it.*] Branwell . . . Branwell . . .

CHARLOTTE. [*Going to her, frightened by her eyes.*] Emily . . . you *must* see a doctor . . . you *must!*

ANNE. Please, Emily . . . please see a doctor.

EMILY. [*Shaking her head.*] Not yet . . . [*A pause as she struggles to catch her breath.*] Charlotte . . .

CHARLOTTE. [*Eagerly.*] Yes, dear?

EMILY. No . . . no . . . not Charlotte . . . [CHARLOTTE *draws back.* EMILY *turns her head toward* ANNE. ANNE *kneels.*] Anne . . . Anne . . . here, in my note-book . . . I wrote . . . a poem the other morning. . . . Perhaps . . . [*She pauses to catch her tortured breath.*]

ANNE. Yes?

EMILY. In it. . . you'll see . . . I said . . . I said that Branwell . . . [*Another pause to catch her breath.*] I said . . . I mean, I gave to him . . .

ANNE. Gave *what*, dear? [*A pause.*] Don't talk if it hurts you. . . .

EMILY. Read it. . . . [*Gives* ANNE *the note-book.*] You'll see then . . . what I mean. . . . I tried to make it plain. Let it go out . . . to prove that he . . . You'll promise? Promise?

ANNE. [*Kneeling beside her, holding her hand.*] Anything, Emily . . . anything.

EMILY. [*Trying to put her hand on* ANNE'S *hair.*] Sweet Anne . . . you're so good . . . *you'll* keep a promise. . . .

ANNE. Of course.

CHARLOTTE. You can't go on like this!

EMILY. Can't I? Oh, yes I can. . . . You don't know how peaceful I feel, Charlotte. . . . No more struggle.

CHARLOTTE. [*Alarmed.*] That means you're giving up. . . . Emily, I'm going for the doctor.

EMILY. [*Weakly.*] Oh . . . have your way again, Charlotte . . . have your way. . . . [*A pause; then whispering it.*] If you'll send for him, I'll see him now.

CHARLOTTE. Now you're speaking sensibly. I'll go for him at once. [*Crossing up to kitchen door.*] Martha!— Martha!

EMILY. It's far to Thornton . . . roads are bad . . . a gig is slow. . . . [*She seems comforted.*]

[CHARLOTTE *in doorway.*]

ANNE. You must go back to bed, Emily. [*Holding her hand, she tries to raise her from the sofa.*]

EMILY. No . . . no . . . not back to bed . . . back to earth . . . that's a nice bed . . . soft heath . . . and sticks and stones . . .

ANNE. Be quiet . . . till the doctor comes.

CHARLOTTE. [*Calling into the hall.*] Martha! Martha!

EMILY. Just open a window for me . . . let in the wind. . . .

CHARLOTTE. The winter wind? That's madness! [*Calling again.*] Martha! Martha!

[MARTHA *hurries in from the kitchen, followed by* TABBY.]

MARTHA. [*Coming down the hall.*] Is anything the matter, Miss Charlotte?

CHARLOTTE. Run quickly . . . to the village, Martha. . . . Fetch a gig. I must go to Thornton. Miss Emily will see a doctor now.

MARTHA. [*Exits center to left.*] Ay, Miss Charlotte.

TABBY. Wot's she runnin' fer? Wot's it about, Miss Charlotte?

[CHARLOTTE *does not reply. She turns back into the sitting-room, going quickly over to* EMILY. TABBY *limps into the room and stands by the door.*]

EMILY. I'll walk a bit with you. . . . Did you blow out the lamp? Good! We'll walk by fire-light, or better in the dark. Don't hold me. . . . Let me go. . . .

CHARLOTTE. But we always walked with our arms around each other, dear.

[*They walk with her, helping her.*]

EMILY. Oh, it was good of you to let in the wind . . . thank you, Anne. . . . Strong wind . . . strong and sweet, with thyme and heather . . . but no . . . but no . . . I swear there's frost in it! [*A gust of wind shakes the house.*] I said I'd walk alone.

[EMILY *shakes herself free from her sisters' detaining hands and walks slowly and feebly down toward the sofa. The wind shrieks.* EMILY *slowly sinks on the sofa and dies without visible struggle. Her head sinks against back of sofa, her eyes remain open.*]

TABBY. [*Crouching. As the gale continues.*] The wind has burst in!

CHARLOTTE. [*Kneeling beside her with a cry.*] Emily!

TABBY. [*Moaning.*] She passed me . . . goin' out with the wind. . . . God rest her where she went.

[TABBY *exits through hallway to left and closes outside door.*]

ANNE [*To* CHARLOTTE *who is trying to find a flutter of* EMILY's *pulse.*] Is she? . . . Is she?

CHARLOTTE. Dead. . . .

ANNE. [*Weeping.*] Our sister . . .

[*The* REV. BRONTË *hurries in from his study across the hall.*]

REV. BRONTË. What's she doing, out of her bed? Disobeying us again?

ANNE. [*Sobbing.*] Oh, Papa . . . Papa . . .

CHARLOTTE. [*With hard, dry eyes.*] Your Emily is at rest, Papa.

[REV. BRONTË *bows his head; then crosses silently and slowly to the sofa. He fumbles out and touches* EMILY'S *cheek. He smooths back her hair.*]

REV. BRONTË. At rest? Has death visited my house again? [*Then gently to* EMILY.] If you find your brother, take care of him, daughter.

ANNE. [*Opening the note-book.*] I promised her . . . What was it I promised? . . . [*She turns the pages. She reads, her lips forming the words but making no sound.*] Oh, Charlotte, what has she done? She's given it to Branwell!

CHARLOTTE. [*Snatching the book.*] Not while *I* still live! [*She reads to herself.*] Oh, no! No! No!

ANNE. If that's published . . .

CHARLOTTE. It shall *not* be published. [*She walks with resolute step to the fireplace.*]

ANNE. [*Terrified.*] Wait, Charlotte! You forget . . . I promised her!

CHARLOTTE. You didn't know *what* you promised.

ANNE. She placed it in my hands. She said . . .

CHARLOTTE. You didn't know.

ANNE. Sh-h-h . . . Wait . . . let me close her eyes first. [*She closes* EMILY'S *eyes.*] There . . . do what you wish. She cannot see.

[CHARLOTTE *tears the poem from the note-book. She crumples it; tosses it into the fire. It smolders; then bursts into flame.*]

ANNE. [*Leaning over* EMILY.] Forgive me, Emily.

[*She kisses* EMILY'S *brow.*]

CHARLOTTE. [*As the poem turns to ashes.*] And anything else that may take away her glory.

THE CURTAIN FALLS

THE END